GUYS LIKE US

GUYS LIKE US

A
MEMOIR
OF
LIFE
LOST
AND
FOUND

SEAN NOLAN

GEMMA

Boston

First published by GemmaMedia in 2011.

GemmaMedia
230 Commercial Street
Boston, MA 02109 USA

www.gemmamedia.com

Printed in the United States of America

15   14   13   12   11   1   2   3   4   5

978-1-936846-01-6

Library of Congress Cataloging-in-Publication Data:

Nolan, Sean, 1974-
    Guys like us : a memoir of life lost and found / Sean Nolan.
        p. cm.
    ISBN 978-1-936846-01-6 (pbk.)
    1. Nolan, Sean, 1974–   2. Nolan, Joseph Michael, 1949–   3. Fathers and sons—New Jersey—Biography. 4. Cycling accident victims—New Jersey—Biography. 5. Amnesiacs—New Jersey—Biography. 6. Nolan family. 7. New Jersey—Biography. I. Title.
    CT275.N6868A3 2011
    974.9'043—dc23
                                            2011017559

Cover by Night & Day Design

For Mike and Kathy and everyone who showed up

CONTENTS

Contents

Chapter 1

THE GOOD PART

"I had an accident. I'm sorry. I don't know who you are."

Joseph Michael Nolan, Jr., former lawyer, former basketball player, former man of the world, stood on the beach in front of his house, shaking hands with another white-haired man who had just introduced himself. His vacant blue eyes took it all in and his distinguished older Irish-American guy hair blew lightly in the breeze, not unlike the man himself these days.

"That's all right, Michael," the man was saying, all the while smiling and shaking his head. At some point, he had said he was a judge, and he began talking excitedly to his wife about who my father was to him, the cases he had worked on, the stories she would know him from, and she was nodding and smiling even more, and the both of them looked a bit like they might cry. "It's just so damn good to see you, Michael. Thought we'd lost you out there." He jerked his head out back inland towards the rest of the island where Route 35 rolled right through the center of our town.

Some people are forever. You know that wherever they are, whether it's been ten minutes or ten years, they'll walk into the room and look and talk and move the same way they did the first time you met them. They barely seem to age, and when they do, it happens so slowly that the next thing you know, they're just gone. You'd swear all day that these people were the measure of your life, your atomic clock. If they barely changed, you seemed all the more different each time you were near them, and they became a thing you could tie yourself to so that maybe you wouldn't change quite so much either.

That's how they saw my father, a thing against which their own lives would be measured. Seeing him so altered, it was hard for them not to linger with him longer than they ever would have before, watching all the new pieces of him fit together.

People were always like this around him now. It had been nearly a year since the accident, and he had been in the hospital most of the time recovering from the head injury that nearly killed him and that totally erased his memory of his entire life. I knew that most of the people who had known him as Mr. Big Shot Lawyer had heard he was dead at first. Then they heard he was dying and then in a coma, and then they stopped hearing anything for months. Then maybe they heard he was locked away in various hospitals, being rehabbed, and then his wife Kathleen hid him away once they let him out, until it could be decided where this man would find his place in the world. Maybe he was in a wheelchair, or drooling on himself in the corner of some expensive rest home in Manhattan.

Since hardly anyone outside of a tight circle of friends and family had seen him for so long, people had a way of going all to pieces when they ran into him. He was a cross between a ghost and some kind of baffling miracle. He was a man not unlike themselves before it all happened, and someone who they had expected for months to finally die, and who had solemnly refused to do so.

It was hard to know who it was harder on now, them or Michael. He at least had the luxury of having no goddamn clue who he was, much less who they were.

"I'm starting to get better," he told them. "I can't ever be a lawyer again. I know that much."

"Heard about that, Michael. I was very sorry about that. We'll miss you. So what will you do now?"

Mike laughed and gestured as if to say 'Here I am, this is where it's at,' and they laughed too.

They walked away in a flurry of smiles, and as they continued on down the beach, looked back in appreciation. We resumed gazing out on the water. It was still hard for him to talk. He used to talk incessantly, yelling or needling or pushing people. Now he could barely put a few sentences together before he had to look up at the sky for the answers.

"I wish I knew myself as well as they do."

"You will, man. It's all going to come back."

It was fitting that this tragedy had played itself out here, 'down the Shore,' as we all called it. Our address was nominally a small town up north where we went to school and the post office delivered our mail and we happened to live for nine months of the year. But it seemed like anything that really happened to us happened here, at the beach where we spent all our summers and many weekends during every other season. This was the place where I learned to ride a bike, to swim, to read, to drink and to fall in love. The Nolans had been coming here for decades, stretching on back to when my grandfather, Joe Nolan, first bought a house when he became A Big Deal. After that initial incursion, the Nolans had infected the place ever since.

Joseph Michael Nolan, Sr., named his first son Joseph Michael Nolan, Jr., and even the names carried a ring of constancy about them, as if the one, looking down on the other, had decided we would just have more of the same, because maybe now we had finally gotten good enough. One went by Joseph and the other by Michael so that you could tell them apart, but even then, sometimes they could not. They were both lawyers, they got each other's mail; they both complained about it and asked you not to mention the complaints to the other guy.

Growing up Nolan, I was spoiled for fairy tales and children's books. There was nothing in the world of unicorns and wild things and hobbits that could really tempt me. I had grown up surrounded by giants. Beyond Joe and Michael was a family that seeped into every aspect of your life, they were that big in my memory.

These Nolans moved around with a fabulous awareness of their own power, and it wasn't power made of money or fame or muscles, mostly it was just personality. Every one of them lit up a room when they walked in, because they were always the loudest and the sweetest and the worst. They drank, they smoked, they pounded the table. Mostly they just laughed at everything, in the best way, a kind word to you when you walked in and a bit of a sneer when you walked by. You knew it, but you didn't really care. People were happy to have their hands shaken with a smile and then asked why they looked like such shit on a swell night such as this, because why not? It was a Nolan asking. They didn't really mean it, did they?

They did. At their core was a solid belief that most other people weren't really that good. They weren't all that good either, but they knew it, and knowing was the thing. I'm no good, you're no good, he's no good, but I'm the only guy willing to say it.

We were all no good. They'd ask you how dumb you were, call you a rotten kid, talk to you like you were twenty when you were just two and then roll their eyes when you couldn't answer and lament how all the brains had run out of this family, we were doomed, going nowhere, this generation was the last. Let's have another. We're it.

"They're not like other people," my mother Kathleen would say, and I think she regarded them the way a doctor did a patient refusing medicine. The Nolans were their own special psychosis, at once self-referential to the point of annoyance and self-deprecating to the point of disbelief. Every story was an exaggeration, every anecdote was over the top and usually involved someone getting what they had coming for messing with one of them.

They belched at tables and emptied liquor cabinets at parties, all the while laughing at themselves and apologizing to no one. "Oh, the hell with it," they'd say, and they meant it. The hell with it, who cares? Not us, that's who. It wasn't long ago that they were in the neighborhoods in Newark with not a lot of money and so it was OK when Aunt Mary raised a glass every Christmas dinner and said "I wonder what the poor people are doing tonight," because when they were kids they said they'd ask that if they ever made it. And they'd made it.

Joe Nolan, the family patriarch and my grandfather, would stand in the corner of the room when we were all together, at birthday parties, or Christmas, and he'd give you a push on the shoulder and whisper conspiratorially, "They're not like everybody else, are they?" It wasn't a question and he didn't talk to you like you were a kid; none of them did. They didn't see age, they didn't acknowledge children. The men would talk to you about their cars, and war, and balls. The women would make you get drinks for them, and don't be a jerk with the pour, get it right this time, damn it.

Michael Nolan, my father, used to try to pretend he was past all of that stuff. He barely drank. He didn't like to party. He didn't glad-hand, he didn't backslap, he never gave a compliment without meaning it, and he never gave them, so you could see where the world fell on his list of things to care about. He knew you were a kid, and when little kids would babble at him, he would lean in, tousle their hair and say "I can't understand a goddamn thing you just said. Come back when you can speak English."

He had one major flaw, and that was that most of the time, he told the truth. It's easy to forget that this is not always a good thing. In school they told us that you should always be honest, tell the truth, don't lie to your mother. He must have taken that to heart at some point, because he had the honesty of a three-year-old.

Michael let people know where they fit in his hierarchy of Things That Matter, and he could be brutal. When you brought home terrible grades, he'd sigh and say something like, "You'll never be Einstein. But Jesus Christ, maybe you can dig a ditch or two someday down the line. It's about the best you're going to do." With these stout words of encouragement, you would troop back to school on Monday and bang your head into the books again. If you complained, if you mentioned that other kids' parents did things differently, he'd have an answer: "That's because other parents think the sun shines out of Little John-ny's ass all day. Get to work."

Here he was, standing next to me on the beach in front of our house, watching the waves on a morning in June. We stood looking out at the water, still cold enough to make you shiver a bit when it hit your legs as it buried them ever so slowly in the sand. I looked back at the house behind us, and then at him and back out at the water. All of this had been waiting on him since he left the house that morning before the accident. There were so many moments when he was lying in one hospital or another when I would wander through his house and look at things of his—his wallet or his watch—lying at his bedside until the day he walked back in that door, months after he thought he would, back on that morning, a summer ago.

He remembered nothing of himself. The accident left him looking the same as he always did, normal in every way. There was barely a scratch on him. Still, when they brought him out of his coma, it was like coming into the world all over again for Mike. That truck gave him a head injury that erased every memory he had ever had. Me and my two sisters, Gwyneth and Michaela, were all strangers to him. Worse than that, so was my mother, Kathleen.

"These people always ask me what I'm going to do with myself. And I wish I had something to tell them. But I've got nothing. I'm nobody now. There's nothing behind me that I could tell anyone."

"I'll tell you anything you want to know."

"What do you know? About me, I mean."

"Honestly, Mike, you were kind of a closed book. But we had some moments."

"Sometimes I think I should just jump in this water and start swimming until I can't go any farther. Maybe if I had died out there on that road, I would have saved everyone a whole lot of trouble. That would have been just all right with me. But since I didn't, here we are. It's got to keep moving. One way or another."

"That's the move, old man. Now you're thinking."

"Tell me about the best day you ever had."

"OK."

That was how it started. Mike wanted to know who he was. All I had for him were the stories I remembered from the times he was around. So whenever he and I got together in the months and years after his accident, that's what we'd talk about, a time when I was a kid that made a difference to me. He had worked hard in his life, and maybe he wasn't exactly the type of guy to volunteer to coach a Little League team, but I wasn't exactly the type of kid who wanted to play Little League anyway. It all worked out.

Chapter 2

FARAWAY YOU

So my dad doesn't speak to me?

No. Not for a long time. He came to the hospital, but we wouldn't let him see you.

Why not?

If he didn't want you in life, he doesn't get you in death. That's the deal.

That's pretty rough. Were you two friends?

Best friends.

When I think about Joe Nolan, I think of the boardwalk at the beach, walking down it by ourselves in the fall, everything all closed up. The summer was for everyone else, that was when the rest of the family was down, staying in one of his houses. In the fall, I would come down on the train or he would come up north to get me. I liked the train, as I preferred anything that allowed me to sit and read for hours with no one asking me to do a thing.

The beach is best in the fall. In the summer, you had to share the place with the rest of the world. The beach was crowded with fat, sweaty, hairy bald men, their oily wives with their shitty beach-reads, and worst of all, their gross children and their amateurish sandcastles built too close to the water. By late afternoon, most people had left and there were just the few stragglers and the isolated empty chairs and tents. Futile moats and walls had turned to lumps of sand.

The summer is hot, and I hate that. I have never understood how people thought it was fun to stick a chair into burning hot sand, and then sit there all damn day in the sun and the heat. By any reasonable measure, this is plainly not fun. During the summer, I prefer to remain inside, or at the very least, on the deck, looking out on the ocean and the beach full of people splayed before it.

Like most places, the beach's summer season was bookended by Memorial Day and Labor Day, only at the beach, you really noticed it. The day before Memorial Day, there would be thirty people on the beach. The day after, you couldn't even see the sand. On Labor Day, the beach is still packed with people down for the day. The very next day, it's deserted.

Some of them will come back for the few weekends in September when you can justify it because the weather is still somewhat warm and the sun is out. But the drop-off is steep, and welcome. The kids in their cars go back up north, and everyone goes back to their jobs.

Sometimes, if I have nothing else to do on a Sunday, I'll catch a train down to the boardwalk in Point Pleasant and sit there on a wet bench, looking at the gray sky and the closed up carnival games. The arcades and pizza joints are still open, but it's lonely, and that's the best part. The only people around are the local kids hanging out, going nowhere, and according to their T-shirts, loving death metal. It feels empty and deserted and lost and rundown and broken, like everyone has forgotten all about it. You know they'll remember again in May, but for an afternoon, it's great to pretend that maybe they won't, maybe they'll never come back, and you can keep it all for yourself.

On a late fall day, years ago, we had gone down to the shore as a family. I was about six or seven. Everyone was reading except Mike, who was out on that porch, working. I had busied myself with a huge stack of comic books I had discovered wedged in between old *National Geographic*s and *Vogue*s on a shelf downstairs. I can still recall their newspapery smell, and the way they got musty when they'd been at the beach for a long time.

When a car pulls up at that time of year, you know it, because out on Ocean Terrace, hardly anyone ever drove by on a lazy, cold

Saturday. I heard the car, and I knew it was Joe Nolan. I also knew he would not have pulled into the driveway, even though there would be plenty of room. There was about thirty feet of Cadillac blocking that street now.

He would make a big display of knocking at the door, so as to be received in the fashion in which he had become accustomed. He'd hung a big crazy doorknocker in the shape of an old captain's head on the door. It was so massive that you couldn't close the screen door very well, so the mesh was all bent outwards. He would bang that ridiculous knocker, and then you'd hear it.

"Hullo! It's Grandpa! Open up! Donuts!"

I would have been running since I first heard the car, having leapt over the couch and slid around at the top of the stairs on that smooth hardwood floor, bounding down the stairs to the front door. He'd be standing there, usually in some horrible old windbreaker that had long since ceased to break anything other than the hearts of those who knew he could afford better, but refused to. That day, though, he was wearing a businessman's raincoat. It was open, revealing green shorts and a hideous yellow shirt the color of puke. When you set it against the bluish gray sky, it evoked seasickness. On top of his head was the ever-present hat that read Captain. He was smiling, and so was I. We both knew what he was here for.

He would make the pretense of having "stopped by"—going upstairs, saying a few things about work to Mike, asking my Mom how the house was, leaving the afterthought donuts in the kitchen. The whole time I would be lurking close by, waiting for the nonchalant, "Well, Kathy, Michael, I was wondering . . . ." he would say, as if the idea had just occurred to him, "maybe Sean and I would go out for the afternoon, see a few things. I have some friends to visit, you know. I could use a . . . *navigator.*" He would say the word and nod his head towards me as if he actually meant I held some sort of rank.

My mom would act surprised. "Well, sure, Joe,"as if she didn't know why he had come from the moment she heard that car.

I would already be halfway through the kitchen and down the stairs with my jacket and my hat, running to the garage to get my sneakers. In Kathleen's house, there were no shoes. Putting them on my feet in mid-stride, I would career out the door and into the driveway, and there it would be, big as a battleship, painted a reflective white that burned the eyes in bright sunlight.

The car.

The word "car" seems inadequate when used describe the great white monster that Joe drove. It's too short and monosyllabic to encompass what, in my memory, has grown to be a vehicle slightly smaller than a tank. To a seven-year-old, this massive Cadillac was like an RV. The front seat was a couch. It had a radio that Joe allowed me to play at volumes inappropriate for either of our ages. Joe washed it twice a week, and the thing was gleaming white, not a scratch on it. The chrome shone even on that day when clouds in the sky threatened snow and the cold air whipped out to the ocean. Joe did not believe in convertibles.

That car was not just his. It was ours. I was consulted when it was time to buy a new one. I helped him clean it; he taught me how. We had a system for washing it. You started with the hood, working your way back. People usually do the roof first, you know, top to bottom. But Joe would say something like, "That makes no difference, I have a garage, there's no pigeon shit on this car." You would think that this was not such a great answer, but you would be wrong. Any other Nolans or friends of his standing nearby would, as always, nod their heads in agreement at this sound bit of thinking.

That car said, "I made it." Back before there were men who felt OK about driving VWs and before the kids with the souped-up Hondas and the "Fear This" stickers, this was a car that said there was a man behind the wheel, and he did not have to tell you what to fear, and God help you if your little foreign car got in his way.

Joe came from a time before cars were everywhere, he remembered when it was a privilege to drive one, when it meant something that you could afford one. Cars were still noble to him. They still conveyed a message beyond a bumper sticker; your car and the way you drove it said something about who you were. He still enjoyed the concept of going out for a drive, something largely lost on most people. Now you get in your car to go somewhere, you don't get in it to putter around aimlessly. When you open the door and turn the key, you have a destination in mind and a route in your head.

Joe and I had neither of these things. He'd show up, we'd get in, and we'd just drive. We could end up anywhere or nowhere. It made you love a car. It was better than a time machine, it was a now machine. You could go anywhere, and you could go right now. It was just out there, sitting in the driveway, and if you were bored, or restless or troubled, you could pull out your keys, hop in, and see anyone, anywhere. That was magic to me. It was the perfect cure for a fidgety, over-anxious kid: a machine that could get you out of here. Later, I collected songs about cars. There was a two-year period in my life when I played "Cadillac Ranch" every morning when I woke up, to the point where, when Mike heard it playing on a weekend, he would stand outside my door until I looked up.

"You're making me hate that song, you know."

Joe and I, everything we did, it seemed like that car was part of it, big and perfect. We took the train to New York once, along with his wife Jeanne and my sisters. It was my first train ride and as the swamps rushed past the window, I can remember Joe leaning over and whispering, "We should have taken the car." I nodded solemnly.

Our drives could take us anywhere, and often enough, they didn't take us all that far, especially when the weather was cold. We ended up in Seaside Heights a lot of the time, walking up and down the boardwalk.

Seaside was a great Jersey town, with just the right aura of sleaze hanging around the place. During the summer, its boardwalk was covered with people who seemed to be going nowhere, all gold chains, perma-tans and cruising along the main drag. There was no shortage of Metallica or Iron Maiden T-shirts, or hair spray or attitude or "Fuck you, pal." There were cheap motels up and down the strip, and the huge beach in front of the boardwalk has been the final resting place for the virginity of many a high school girl from North Jersey.

The boardwalk was covered in people twenty-four hours a day. At first glance, driving by, you'd think it was a great place for families. You'd see rides and water parks and the huge Ferris wheel on which

Dick Eaton puked all over Mom's competition for Mike's affection in high school, Sally Thorpe. You'd think this might even be a good place to bring the kids someday. You'd be wrong.

Once you got up onto the boardwalk, you'd realize all that stuff was only camouflage for the bars and drunks and overgrown children that inhabited the place. Grown men, spilling out of the open air bars, fell down drunk. Teenagers threw pizza at one another and got served beer, no questions asked. Girls' hair was big here, and the guys rocked enough hair gel to render them bulletproof. Everyone had a cigarette dangling from their mouth, even the kids.

That day we drove to Seaside. If there is one thing the old man respected, it was a bit of character around a place.

Safely out on the highway, he asked me, "Wanna drive?"

I climbed up and grabbed the wheel, steadying myself and pulling my head up so I could see over the horizon hidden by the dashboard. The only instrumentation I understood was the speedometer; the rest of it all looked like the dials and gizmos from science fiction movies.

We pulled out onto Route 35. Thirty-five mph in the summer to increase the ticket revenue from tourists, forty-five mph the rest of the year to allow us to make it to Seaside in fifteen minutes. We rode through Ortley Beach, Lavalette, Ocean Beach—little towns with little houses and businesses that existed only in the summer. There might be a restaurant or a gas station here and there to serve the locals during the winter, but there were only a few people around. The streets were wet and sandy from the wind blowing in off the ocean, and everywhere it smelled like wood burning from the chimneys, mixed with the tang of the sea and the salt, and I wish I could bottle that up and take it with me whenever I am anywhere else. That smell gives me a feeling in my chest like I want to stay out all night.

We pulled into the big empty parking lot across from the Whistlestop Café, which would one day become the site of my ill-fated two-week career as a fry cook, during which I would burn myself no fewer than twenty times.

Usually we would just walk up and down the boardwalk, bullshitting. Sometimes we would go and play one of the old-time games like skee ball in the arcades that stayed open year round. There was hardly anybody in the place other than the old man leaning against the corner who gave you your change and a few kids standing around in hoodies.

We talked. It was cold, and soon it started to snow. I suppose it is one of those landscapes that only people who grew up there think of as beautiful—the skeletal Ferris wheel hulking over the beach, the boarded-up doors and windows, the greenish gray water churning behind you, the silent rides waiting for summer and the kids huddled in the doorways against the snow. It was such perfect, happy loneliness in a place meant to be full of so many and yet so empty of everything.

Joe's father John was from Ireland. Whenever it was cloudy or rainy or snowy, I would ask him, "Is this like Ireland?" and he would say, "Yes, but not as green" or "not as cold" or "not as pretty" or something. Wherever we were was never as good. The weather was never as good, the people were never as good, the beer was never as good.

"So Ireland is like Heaven or something?" I asked.

He laughed against the snow. "That's what they want you to think, the ones from over there. Everything was always better than here, that's what they say." We sat down on a bench looking out at the water. "But the people feeding you that are the ones that left, aren't they?"

Somewhere along the way our conversations ruined me for kids my own age and for most adults. He never spoke to me as a boy. He spoke to me like I was anyone else. Nothing was ever softened up for me; he would tell me what he thought. He'd discuss the intricacies of his cases at work with me, although I had no idea what he was talking about and he knew it. We would talk about friends of his. He didn't like old people much, and although I considered him to be old*er*, he was never old in the sense that I thought of old people back then. Old people to me were those likely to be dying soon. His friends all lived like they were in their twenties, talking about cars and broads and booze.

We would walk and talk. I would tell him about school—complaints about math and science ("Cash is King. You'll need math to count all your cash. How will you count your cash with no math?") and the other kids ("You don't wanna play baseball, don't worry about it. They don't play baseball at Notre Dame.")

He fancied himself a great advisor, but really, there was very little advice given. I babbled about the things that seemed important to me, mostly having to do with teachers I didn't like or kids that didn't like me. That day I was telling him about teachers at my new school. There was this one art teacher, Mr. Gillis, with a really bad Jersey accent. He never knew any of our names, everyone was just "Kid," as in, "Hey, kid. Come here, ya leaving all dis paint on da flah for someone ta trip on, damn it. Ders gonna be some listenin' here, or someone's getting' da horns. Dat's right—ya mess wit da bull, ya get da horns."

"Well, I would say this to the man. 'What,' I would ask him, 'does anyone from New Jersey know from bulls or horns anyhow? Or art? Or anything?'"

There was Mr. Cross, who had been partly raised in Scotland. He was a soccer coach, and at school we'd all laugh, because he'd be singing in this Scottish accent while he took a piss. Only that's not the weird thing. The weird thing is that he wouldn't just pull his shorts down a little to wiz, or use the convenient opening at the front. This cat would stand in front of the urinal with his pants totally down around his ankles. He would do this and be singing "Girls Just Wanna Have Fun" at the same time. It was totally weird.

Joe shook his head: "Presbyterians, yeah."

At the end of the boardwalk was the trashiest of all the trashy bars, the Sawmill. It had a giant cartoon buzz saw on the top of it cutting through a log, and it was made up to look like a log cabin. It was one of those places that when you walked by as a kid, you instinctively knew to stay away. The crowd was rough, and there were always big Harleys parked near it on the street. In contrast to the heavy metal T-shirts and gold-chain-and-mousse crowd, the people in the Sawmill wore a lot of leather, even the women. Especially the women.

Still, you were curious. The clientele was awful-looking. Some had no teeth, some had missing limbs and black eyes and what appeared to be fresh facial lacerations. In the cold, I imagine it was worse, because it was a really distilled bunch in there—the bad weather boiled away the hangers-on, so you only had the finest biker drunks available. The jukebox played eighties hair bands or Southern rock, and we figured there was a standing regulation that the Allmans or Mötley Crüe were to be played on the hour.

But the people in the place were always laughing hysterically, no matter when you walked by. Smoke poured from the place like it was on fire, beer bottles regularly fell out the windows, the walls of the joint appeared to move because of the number of people stuffed inside it—it may have been the busiest establishment for miles around. Through the windows and in through the open door, a nonstop party could be seen in full swing any time.

Snow was coming down, and we were walking past the place. Like most people, we stopped and stared, trying to catch a glimpse of the mayhem we thought and hoped might be going on in there. In the far parking lot, I could see bikes all lined up in front of the boardwalk, and there was this dingy light coming from the inside. The front door was always open, no matter what the weather, and you could see people playing pool and drinking inside. I looked at them in their leather and their long hair with their Coors Lights and Budweisers. They looked back, a few of them raising a beer in our general direction.

And then the yelling started. She was a big fat woman in a jean jacket with wild red curly hair and a face like a tree trunk, staggering out of the place, flailing some, but managing to keep her feet.

"Hey old man! Hey old man!" She teetered and she swayed, and now the big rough characters with scarred faces and unkempt hair were looking. "Are you a flasher? HUH? Is that what you are, a flasher?"

I looked at Joe, and, sweet shit, she was right. In this light the pukey shirt and executive rain jacket and shorts combo made him look exactly like some flasher. He must have looked like an old pervert. I was nervous. More people were slowly walking out of the bar, pointing and laughing and nudging one another. But I looked at Joe, and he was smiling back. He seemed unafraid, in his element even. I could see no reason for this. I did not relax.

Joe began walking towards the bar, and I thought, well this is it, we'll be in the paper tomorrow in the sad story section Mom always read aloud in the mornings and people will hear about the terrible beating of a young boy and his grandfather and say things like, "Isn't it a shame about Seaside? It used to be such a NICE place," and I would be thinking the same thing while I learned to walk again over the coming months. The fat lady was still smiling and yelling, "Here comes the flasher!"

I followed somewhat timidly behind him as the length and breadth of the Sawmill and all its ragged glory filled my entire field of vision. For whatever reason, Mötley Crüe was no longer playing. Frank Sinatra's "Summer Wind" was blaring out across the boardwalk, into the snowy air, and it could not have come at a better time.

As we got close, Joe pulled open the jacket to the applause of the patrons who had watched the beginning of the scene. The laughter from them grew to roars, and I moved slowly away.

Closing the jacket, Joe began to dance this strange little dance by himself in time to the music, back and forth, moving his legs like scissors, slowly, like a crazy Irish Astaire in the snow. He whirled around in his sneakers across the boardwalk, eyes vacant like he was listening to some other music somewhere, moving like he wasn't himself, drifting across the wood almost like the snow. I think he might have moonwalked. More people were noticing now, coming out of the bar to see this bizarre old man, and there was general hooting and hollering and clapping from the drunks as Joe slapped his heels with his hands and, removing his cap, saluted them and ended his little dance. They loved it.

The big fat woman ran out and hugged him and slapped me on the back. "He's some flasher," she said in a shrill, witchlike voice. I looked up at him, smiling back at them as they all waved him in.

We were received into the bar, led by the crowd of well-wishers who clearly thought this was the greatest thing they'd seen all year. The place smelled like a cigarette butt put out in an old beer, but it was warm in there, and the laughter was infectious. That day, I began to see why people liked bars so much, despite how horrible the bar itself or anyone inside it looked. This was a great place to be, and even at seven years old, I knew this beat the arcade any day. I wanted to be one of these people, not exactly like them, but I wanted to be having this kind of fun all the time, they way they did, the way they played loud music and guffawed at everything.

We were given two seats at the bar as everyone came up to shake Joe's hand and laugh and ask me my name. Joe introduced me to all these strangers he had won over. One man came up to him and said, "You're the fucking king, Joe!" All the women wanted to dance with him and the men just thought this was hysterical. They called me "Little Man," like Joe did. Two beers were put down in front of us; I instinctively reached for the glass. Joe tapped my arm, gave me a look and said, "None for you . . . you're driving."

I sat on the bar stool and talked to everyone, or so it seemed. They talked to me like I was anyone else, anyone but a seven-year-old lost in a big person's world that day. At some point, I looked over and saw Joe Nolan along with so many others dancing in front of the jukebox, coat flapping, arms waving, and for the life of me, I can hardly remember what it was, but a reggae song came on and it was like New Year's Eve in there. Everyone was dancing and I could hardly see him. I stood up on my stool to see more of him, just to watch what he did, he was so full of something good that day, but I still couldn't see him, so I stood on the bar. The whole place was drunk at three in the afternoon and there were conga lines and the reggae music was so loud, and now I could see him, dancing with everybody in the joint. But I was just fine where I was on the bar. Looking down at my hand I could see someone had put a small glass of beer in it, and I lifted it up in the air like it was the Olympic Torch and stood there in the weak light and loud music of a snowy winter Sunday in that bar and thought how lucky I was.

MASSIVE NIGHTS

How did you find out about me? Who called you?

Michaela. *Slight pause.* Your daughter. The morning after an insane night before.

Did you bring your friends?

In a way.

How was that night before?

Santa Claus gotten beaten up. That's all you really need to know, except there's more.

I imagine this has to do with your dipshit friends.

A guy like you should know the value of the kind of friends who would drop everything for you.

If you're going to beat up Santa Claus, you'd better have a good reason.

It was five o'clock on a Thursday night, and I'd already staked out some real estate at the bar. The name of the place referenced insanity, and I'd say most nights a good ten percent of the joint qualified. By the end of the night it would be closer to ninety.

Paul the bartender had a wonky arm and was from Ireland. I said the wonky arm part because you'd notice that first just looking at him. He also claimed to be Jewish, and he would often approach you at some ungodly hour when you were ten pints into the night to ask if you thought he was the only Irish Jew currently within a ten block radius. 'Fifty," you'd say, and then he'd cackle and expose you to the failures of Irish dentistry.

The place itself was the definition of the word *nondescript*. There was nothing on the walls other than bumps and pukey green paint. Years ago, there had been a clock on one wall that said "Irish Times" on it, but Paul could never decide whether to keep it to New York time or Dublin time, so he threw it out.

The tables were half a foot too short, so your legs never really fit under them. The chairs were from a different time when people were smaller and hemp rope seemed like a really good thing to make furniture out of.

Out back, there was a big yard with a mural of New York around it, the kind with people on the sidewalk all looking back at you. It was the smoking section, and that was fine, except for the big oxygen canisters sitting close by to power the outdoor heaters. If there's ever a small mushroom cloud hanging somewhere in the vicinity of Tompkin's Square Park, you can bet that someone lit up a bit too close to those things.

I hate getting to a place before everyone else, but with Paul being a good friend, I never really minded here. He had the same songs on his iPod as my friends and I had, which makes you a friend nowadays. We'd sit there and bullshit about whatever was new, and on that night I was telling him about my thoughts on the naming of bands and probably boring the shit out of him. He couldn't have been that disinterested because he was ignoring everyone else at the bar waiting for a drink. He made a habit of this, and his brother did, too. They had a very Irish understanding of capitalism, which generally goes like this: "Let the bastards wait. I may have a service and they have money, but these things will be exchanged according to my schedule. If they don't like it, well . . . fuck them."

Jack walked into the bar, shaking his head. He and Paul exchanged "Hey, mans" and then said, "Ahhhhhhh, maaaaaan."

"What's up? Good day? Bad day?"

"Excellent day."

"What happened?"

"I don't even know how to say this, so I'm just going to say it. I was told a fantastic story about our friend Kevin last night. For your listening pleasure, I am willing to tell you the entire thing."

By now, I was laughing. Jack was holding his head in his hand, rubbing his eyes, looking around wildly—all his usual theatrics whenever something had happened—only he rarely did it all at once.

"OK, so?"

"Brian beat the hell out of a department store Santa Claus."

"Are you serious? That can't be. We would have heard about it."

"It happened. He beat the shit out of a Santa. Think about what I am saying to you. Think about it very hard. We KNOW a guy who beat up a guy dressed up as Kris Kringle."

Paul knew Kevin. If you knew him, you knew that this wasn't a joke, or an exaggeration or a lie. He was completely capable of this sort of thing. Not only was he able, but it was probable during any given year that he would do this sort of thing at least two or three times. He wasn't a thug so much as he was drunk and ill-tempered. That may sound like the same thing, but he always seemed to feel bad about the terrible things he did once they were described to him the next day.

A sample conversation with him would go something like this:

You: "Hey, man."

Him: "Did I tell you about the four-foot-ten Chinese girl I took home this weekend?"

You: "No."

Him: "Sorry, man. I meant to ask how work was going."

You: "Work's good."

Him: "Did I tell you about the four foot ten Chinese girl I took home this weekend?"

He was not for everyone.

"Tell me this story. How did this happen?"

Paul put Jack's pint down in front of him, both guys laughing. "Allow me to continue. Allow me to start from the beginning. His cousin asked him to bring her kids to the mall to see Santa a few days ago. He says yes because he says yes to everything this broad asks him to do, like the rest of the family, without thinking. Only he was out drinking with another cousin all night, and they get home at, like, six in the morning. She wakes him up at nine to drive them to the mall, and he's barely moving."

"This kid once slept on a hardwood floor with a chair leg as a pillow. I can't believe he got up."

"The guy must have smelled like the floor of a bar after a drunk pissed himself. I bet his hair was all greasy and everything. Like a big drunk bear."

Jack continued. "So this disgusting animal gets up, picks up his keys, and drives these two screaming kids to the mall. Have you seen these kids? They're like a J. Crew commercial, dressed up and well behaved, and here's this fat drunk driving them to the mall to see Santa, probably weaving all over the road. Merry Christmas.

"They get there, and there's, like, two hundred parents in line with screaming kids, and it's still early. Kevin sees this and starts freaking out. He's hungover, he stinks, he can't have a smoke, and he's got these two kids pulling all over him. And he sees the line and knows it's going to keep going on for hours."

"Or until he beats up the fat man," I said.

"Oh, no. He waits it out. He makes it up to the front. And by the time he makes it up there, there's another two hundred people behind him, all waiting to take a picture with Santa."

At this point, a hipster leans over the bar waving a twenty dollar bill and asks Paul if he's the bartender and can he get a little service.

"Fuck off."

I watched the guy leave and then looked back at Jack. "I sense we're getting to the ugly part?"

"Yeah, this is where it gets bad. His niece and nephew go up to see Santa. One of these ridiculous adults dressed up like an elf is there to take the picture, along with, like, ten other elves. The niece gets up on Santa's lap, and as this happens, Kev steps up to take a picture of his own, the guy remembered his camera even in the midst of his befuddlement. One of the elves puts his hand over the camera and tells him he can't take a picture, that all pictures need to be paid for. Kevin goes insane."

"Like?"

"He charges Santa like a bull. Knocks down the elf helping to lift the kid and punches Claus right in the face. He and Santa go tumbling off of the Santa throne and knock over the entire North Pole backdrop. The whole time, Kevin is flailing away at the guy. Pandemonium breaks out, kids are screaming, moms are screaming . . . DADS are screaming. The place goes nuts, there's two hundred kids, a week before Christmas, watching some thug beat the snot out of Santa, and every one of them starts crying at once; it's like a bomb going off.

"At one point, an elf tries to pull Kev off of Santa, but he bitchslaps the elf. The elf goes down, and now this psycho is strangling Santa with his own fake beard. You can imagine the scene. It's a horror movie, and our friend is Freddy Krueger."

"So how did they stop him?"

"Mall security. It took four of them to pull him off. When the cops tried to put him in the car, he was still holding Santa's fake beard in his hand. Yeah, that's how it went down."

Paul finally broke in. "So, how did you hear this?"

"He was asking me how my day was going, and then he just sort of mentioned it. I mean, who would have ever thought to ask if he'd ever beaten up a Santa?"

At this we lost it. Even Paul, the quietest Irish person I'd ever met, nearly put beer out through his nose. "Did they take him to the police station?"

"Yes."

"What was that like?"

"The cops were unhappy, to say the least. B's brother went up to the sergeant. He calls in a few of the other cops, and now it's a firing squad, these guys all throwing questions at him. Is this the kind of person with which you choose to associate? You know this guy's an animal? You know my kid thinks Santa's dead and Christmas isn't coming because of you people? You know Santa's gonna be in the hospital for Christmas, you piece of garbage?"

"That's the worst thing he's ever done."

"Is it? I don't know. He hit a guy in the face with a shovel once.

He lights bags of crap on old people's doorsteps. He took a shit on a swan in the park. I don't know if this is a new low, or if this is just how things are, and we haven't been paying attention."

We reflected on this for a minute, the three of us staring at different parts of the ceiling, letting the shame sink in good and deep.

Paul spoke first.

"Beer, lads?"

I did my best to avoid sunlight and sleep, so the bars of New York City became like second homes. I could no more leave them than I could walk to Central Park and put out a towel and lay in the sun. If I've ever preferred a view, it's from the back of dark bar out the window to a streetscape of active, happy, chattering passersby, walking with each other in the sunlight. I imagine they look into bars at that hour and see people like ourselves and talk about us like we're an exhibit at the zoo. And then again, sometimes I think they probably don't talk about us at all.

There was a bar down the Jersey Shore with a sign hanging in it that read, "Like We Do." I always took to that; it was like an inside joke. You may come to visit, but this place, the people in it, this is our thing. This is how we get down. And any bar I spent a lot of time in, I thought of that. Looking out the window at the people walking by, I'd think they were clearly not as clever as us, as we'd made arrangements in scheduling and lifestyle that enabled us to be here, right now, in this bar, while they were out doing things, the likes of which I could not even bring myself to imagine.

One night in Tasmania, in such a bar, I met a man who had lost his wife a few years before. They had planned to travel the world together when he retired, but she died too soon. She never made it. He was carrying a picture of her in a frame with him on his journey around the world that he made alone. He and I spent the whole night drinking, and he told me about every single place he had taken her picture. It's things like that you'd miss if you stayed home, because you never know who's in the bar when you're not there.

Thinking that made me feel guilty if I stayed home. Living in New York made me feel guilty if I stayed home. The lameness of my apartment made me feel guilty if I stayed home. So I went out a lot.

More of our friends kept arriving.

Our crowd soon took up almost half the bar, and walking through groups or standing in one place, I'd hear snippets of conversation which grew to form a long, uninterrupted song of nonsense. Some of it I'd heard before, some of it was new, some of it I never wanted to hear again.

Stories broke over me as I moved through the crowd and it swirled around me. Our stories, the stories from the people around us, the good, the stupid, the ridiculous. I'd stop and hear one, move along, tell another, overhear some more, order another drink and come back to something else entirely.

". . . and my buddy Nick is in the local downtown Lucky Strike this past Mother's Day about six beers deep . . . at two p.m. All of a sudden, guy realizes his fiancé's wallet has been stolen out of her purse. So our hero pieces together that the perpetrator was likely a random girl with white sunglasses that had been hanging around their lane. Calls the bank, cancels the credit cards, and they say the card has just been used to buy seventy-five dollars worth of White Castle two blocks away.

"He goes tearing out of the bowling alley alone. Grabs a cop on the sidewalk and tells him to 'call for backup.' Arrives at White Castle first and goes bursting in the door as White Sunglasses and her boyfriend are walking out the door. Hero gets in their face and starts a scuffle as five cop cars pull up, lights blazing, parking on the sidewalk like they're arriving at a bank robbery. The perps drop the food, our guy is barking orders to cops, and the cops chase the perps down the street with the associated tackling and handcuffs.

"A fight over lack of proof breaks out. Thinking quickly on his feet, he gets the register tape from White Castle with his fiancé's name on it. Hands it to the cops. Case closed. They book the crooks and take them downtown. Justice and White Castle are served. Guy picks up the dropped bag of food . . . bought with his money . . . and starts eating a burger. The best part? A cop looks down and mentions our hero is still wearing his bowling shoes. Asks how's his frame is going. Walks back into Lucky Strike and finishes his frame rolling a far and away personal record of 190 . . ."

". . . see, *The Searchers* is easily his most underrated movie. That's my opinion, which should mean everything to you. If he'd have made a samurai movie, it would have been the best samurai movie. If he'd have made an alien movie, it would have been the best alien movie. But he didn't. He made a cowboy movie. Do you see what I'm saying? He was the best. That is what I'm saying. That is my statement . . ."

". . . the Jets, yeah, the Jets. It's so dishonorable to switch teams in the middle of life, but do you ever wish you could? Just once I'd like to see my team go to the Super Bowl. I'd pay whatever it took to get there. But this team, it may never happen. I'm thirty-three years old, and it's never ever happened. I don't think I can die this way, I really don't. But I might . . ."

". . . the band is together now. Jimmy's back on drums, Clare's on guitar and with the tits and all, it's good for the front row crowd. The only thing left is the name. I was thinking of calling ourselves The Nuclear Awesome. Too braggy? We might not be awesome at first. Bonesy thinks the best thing is to be Someone and the Somethings. Like Mo Shittles and the Wasteband Factory or Henry and the Headless Mistress or Jack Shat and the Bullet-Riddled Messengers. Totally inane things like that. We could change it every night, every night have a different name, only each time it would be that same variation on Johnny Whoever and the Whatevers. Our legion of fans would have to follow the papers to see where we were going to be playing based on the name . . ."

". . . we're at the Cuckoo's Nest in Hoodside, Queens last night. Regular Woodside bar basically filled with Irish people. Not a hard-core menacing place like Saints 'n Sinners, just regular people. Anyway, there is, of course, a dude in there still wearing his construction gear—orange vest, helmet, light on top of the helmet. He must have been a train tunnel guy or something. The guy was wasted.

"We were sitting at a table by the door. He walks up to the table and pulls out rolling papers and a dime bag and goes, 'Do you guys party? This shit is on the house.' Guy is rolling a joint in the middle of the bar. This is at, like, eleven p.m., not three a.m. He goes, 'This is good stuff; my friend grows it for me.'

"I then asked where he grew it—in the closet perhaps? 'In the closet? Half my boy's house is kind buds!' At this point, an Irish girl who is sitting at the bar saw what he was doing and told him to stop. The girl had a pretty thick Irish accent; anyone not retarded would know this. He turns to her and goes 'Where you from, Minnesota?' She says yes, and smiles, and he goes, 'Oh yeah, well I am from Woodside, born and raised. I am IRA, I dunno 'bout you, SO GO BACK TO MINNESOTA.' Clearly, he is quite down with the IRA . . ."

". . . I wanna go crazy with you. This is what I say to her. I wanna leave these California health plates, go back to my joint, and stare at each other . . ."

". . . There's a few great words we need to bring back, and top of the list? Top of the list is 'fink.' What a great word. 'That guy finked and we all went to jail,' how cool does that sound? Fink . . ."

". . . happened to be speaking with cousins about an uncle's death last November—I missed the wake and funeral because I was on my way to the Dominica for a wedding. Seems my cousin Chris, who you may remember as the perpetually intoxicated fifty-year-old seaman bachelor poet, showed up at the wake with a Chinaman, both wearing suits. Since no one recognized the Chinaman, and since Chris is not gay, eyebrows were raised. Inquiries were made. Turns out Chris had hired his Chinese delivery guy to drive him the thirty minutes to and from the wake, insisting, of course, that he wear a suit. To show respect. A phenomenal drunk . . ."

". . . the next morning I make us breakfast, and she asks if I'm gay. I ask why, she says it's gay to make a girl breakfast. So I throw it in the garbage and ask who's gay now? She never called back . . ."

". . . you missed a classic night at Keenan's. Drunks slumped over their drinks. Dominican girls using four-letter words every fifth word. A guy in a yarmulke. A dead-ringer for the one-armed man from *The Fugitive* arguing with his lady friend. A cover band that played Merle Haggard and Randy Newman. An old-timer who regaled us with the tale of Polish Night at Yankee Stadium circa 1985, when there was a double tag out at home plate, with the second out being 'Boo-Boo Berra,' who I took to be Dale. And, in case you were wondering, he said Phil Niekro was dancing the polka with twenty Polish broads . . ."

It was time to go. I was supposed to get to the Jersey Shore the next day, and I had no car, of course. I dialed Robbie. It was the only number besides my own that I knew anymore. The only reason I knew it was because we'd been friends since we were kids and he'd moved into his parents' house when they died. Their number in Bloomfield was the same as it had been thirty years before.

"Robbie."

"Hey, man."

"I'm OK. I'm in the city."

"Course you are."

"Think I can get a car in Hoboken?"

"Yeah. Of course. Not a problem. Gimme an hour."

"Cool."

"Listen, I ain't seen you in a while. I'll drop it off myself."

"You don't have to do that."

"See you in an hour."

I walked past them all, hearing nothing now. I didn't have any legs anymore. Outside, the street felt like a foreign country. Then I saw the cabs on the avenue and it felt like home again when I got in. Take me to Jersey, man. Fifty bucks? How much? You're kidding. OK.

The cabbie told me he was from Ghana, and I did what I always do, which is to lie and tell them my father had been in the foreign service in whatever country they were from; he had reported that both the people and the country were beautiful. This was the furthest thing from true, as my father would never have gone to any of the places that most cab drivers were from, even though most of them probably were just fine.

In Hoboken, the girls were trashier and the dudes were bigger, and that's just the way Jersey is and I like it. I bought the *Post* and waited for Bobby in a New Orleans-themed bar for some reason. I ordered a Hurricane, like we do, and looked out the window at the street. Presently, a car pulled up and Robbie stepped out.

He never disappointed. He dressed the part—black suit, black tie, black shirt, an air of menace and a face that never smiled. Our friendship ran deep, and the families knew one another from way back when, which in towns like Verona and Bloomfield and West Orange meant "back in Newark when we all lived there." Family legend had it that someone in our family had done a favor for someone in his family, back when one of them controlled a piece of the action down on the docks. There was speculation that this involved a blind eye when the Bad Thing had been done at some point, but nobody knew for sure. We just knew that there was a debt back there somewhere, but it was never uncomfortable and never spoken about.

As a kid, Bobby beat the shit out of a lot of other kids, most of whom had it coming and some of whom I'd have loved to have had the pleasure to beat myself. He did it less out of joyful sadism and more in a resigned "you will respect me" sort of way.

I walked out to meet him as he stood waiting on the cobblestoned street. Robbie was a relic from another time and maybe the last of his breed. He nodded when he saw me and threw the keys my way.

"She's yours."

"Thanks, man. I'll have it back to you this weekend."

"Whenever."

"How's business?"

"My business is always good. How's yours?"

"Boring as hell. I'm headed down the Shore tomorrow. Shouldn't be but a day."

"Ain't been in years. Wasn't really my scene." This was true, insofar as it went, but Robbie's scene was more likely to be the strip clubs and dive bars along places like Highway 9 and Route 22 than anywhere else. It occurred to me that his work hours likely started right about now.

"Can I drop you off?"

"Nah. I get around, as they say."

"Thanks again. I owe you one."

"No, you don't. See you around."

He walked off towards a parking lot, and I watched him get into the back of a black car that slowly pulled away. The scene made me a little sad. I liked Robbie, I wished we saw more of one another, but I remembered a conversation my old man and I had one day before I started high school. Always stay friends with a guy like that, but don't stand too close. I didn't want to feel like I'd used him, like he just came in handy in a pinch, but the truth is, he did. A guy like Robbie was good to have around. I guess maybe I was good for him, too. His life didn't strike me as particularly full of people he could trust who didn't ask for much.

The car was almost too nice, too brand new. For a second, I had to think of which way I was going, where to start and where it ended. When I pulled out onto the street, I left a little rubber and made a little noise. It was good to be back home.

Chapter 4

RETURN TO ME

They've told me *how* it happened, but I don't get *why* it happened.
Why did I even start riding that bike? If I was such a mean guy,
why would I ride a bike? All I hear about is how much I worked and
how I was never around. Who had time to ride a bike?

You'd get obsessed with things, Mike. This was just the latest. It was
always something. You always did everything over the top. Some
guys blow lots of money on cars. You rode your bike. It kept you
young.

It nearly killed me.

Nearly. Yeah.

Mike took forty-mile bike rides every Sunday. He and his next-door
neighbor at the beach, Marty Jacobs, would get up at six in the
morning and hit the road, biking up Routes 34 and 35 from Normandy
Beach all the way up to Asbury Park, which in my mind is too goddamn far to drive, much less bike. He was nearly fifty-five years old,
and this seemed like fun to him. To me it just seemed like one more
thing he was into that he could count me right out of, which was probably half the reason he did it.

The bike was the one normal-guy-with-a-hobby thing he had going for himself. As hard as he worked, he rarely spent anything on
himself. His car was ten years old, an old Ford SUV, out of place in
the parking lots at the law firms he had to visit. He bought suits for

himself, but those were the tools of the trade. Everything else he had, he had because someone else wanted it: the kids, or Kathy, or the office. The bike was his only thing, and he had come to it late in life. I bought him Flann O'Brien's *The Third Policeman* because of the part about people riding bikes so much that they become half people and half bicycle, thinking maybe he would get the joke. He didn't. "Do you ever read these books before you give them to people? Because they're not good."

Mike's bike had arrived without fanfare at the beach house. One afternoon, Kathy answered the door to find two surfer types in sunglasses standing on the porch with a bike that looked like it had come from the future. She had no idea about any bike, she said. They asked for Mike, and when he appeared, there were high-fives all around. They came in and proceeded to talk to him for an hour about the bike, how they had customized it for him, the little extras he'd paid for, how much he was going to love it. This was obviously not their first time talking bikes with Mike Nolan. Kathy stood there dumbfounded the entire time, wondering how any of this had happened, and perhaps like me from time to time, wondering how well she really knew him. It never ceased to amaze any of us: people who did not know him that well really liked him.

"Your husband is wild awesome, Mrs. Nolan. He knows his bikes. Nice." With that, they left, leaving behind not only the bike, but a ton of accessories, including, unfortunately, a few pairs of tight biker pants. The questions flew at him while he moved everything into the garage. When did you decide to buy this? How much did all this cost? When did all this start? When would you find time to ride a bike with your schedule?

The truth was, Mike didn't know. I wound up asking the same questions, and he never had any answers. But for Kathy, he thought he owed her something. "Well, Lance Armstrong, you know." That's no kind of answer, she'd said. "Lance and I both hate the French," he'd said. "That's as good as I've got."

Now he had something, the first thing he'd really been into outside of basketball and the law. We called it the Third Phase, and to our

way of thinking, maybe this would be what he'd pursue if he ever lived
to retire. Maybe he'd take Kathy over to see the Tour de France every
year, and maybe he'd do a little amateur racing himself. You could
never tell. Once he got into something, he tended to get all into it.

When I would call down to the house on weekends, I'd go through
the motions of asking where he was for a while, usually expecting to
hear that he was called away to the office, and Kathy would say how
he was away on the goddamn Lance Armstrong bike. He'd come in,
sweating like hell, an intense look on his face, like he might punch
two holes through the ceiling and start doing pull-ups if everyone
wasn't careful.

"How was the ride, old man?"

"Fucking great. What have *you* done today?"

The phone had been ringing for a while when I finally separated
my face from the pillow. It was too early for the phone to ring on a
Sunday. I was on the couch. The windows were open. The coffee table
had beer bottles and an ashtray on it. The TV was on, showing replays
of yesterday's ball games. I was still wearing my jeans. It was warm
out, but I could tell by the light that it was still very early and I had
not slept long. The phone was still ringing.

My sister's name was displayed on the phone. I did what I always
did when someone called too early and I was not sure how my voice
would sound after smoking a pack of cigarettes, I repeated: Hey, how
are you? three times before answering, "Hey, how are you?"

She was talking about Route 35 and bicycles and some truck and a
head injury and the name of a hospital. It was hard to wrap my brain
around it all. Mike had been hit by a truck while riding his bike, and
I knew it was grab-your-shit-and-get-down-here bad from the little
tremble in her voice.

"How bad does it look?"

"Really bad. His head is all messed up. It looked so awful."

"Is he going to die?"

"I think so."

"Where is he?"
"They took him in the helicopter. Get here quick."
"OK."

I stopped for a second and regarded the empty bottles and the full ashtray in front of me: there's been an accident. Someone ran him over on Route 35 while he was on his bike. His head is torn up good. He's an hour-and-a-half-drive away down at a hospital in Neptune, New Jersey.

On the way down the stairs I called a friend in the State Police. I let her know I would be coming down the Turnpike and the Parkway at great speed, could she ring ahead to make sure I didn't get pulled over, so I would get there before the old man died. Sure, she said, asking for nothing more than confirmation about the make of the car so she could call it in. Cops are cops.

I remember every second of that drive. I remember the turn out of Hoboken and onto the ramp through Jersey City, the sun shining off of the skyscrapers and the empty road in front of me. I came down the ramp onto the Turnpike and the road was still clear, just a few cars here and there, all of which I was flying past. I was the fastest thing on the road that morning; I blew past every single living thing in New Jersey. There was hardly anyone on the highway, and I pushed that car the whole way.

I concentrated on driving, trying to keep my head clear of any thoughts about the enormity of what could be happening today. If I did that, if I pondered the idea that Mike Nolan might turn out to be just another human after all, it could come apart, and I just needed to get there. I didn't know anything yet, I told myself. All I had was my stupid sister telling me what she thought she saw on the road. She thought he might die, she thought his head looked bad. I've seen a lot of injuries that look bad, and they turn out to be nothing. If I thought about it, I'd have to slow down; I'd have to notice things. There was no time to notice anything. The important thing was to be there. "Get there," I repeated to myself. "Just get there."

Only once, pulling onto the Parkway from the Turnpike, did the situation creep in. I remembered being at that toll plaza, sitting in the old man's Ford Thunderbird—not the old-timey cool one, the horrible 1980s incarnation—when he turned down a Springsteen song to tell me that the Parkway was Thunder Road, did I know that? Most people didn't know that, he said. I had no idea if it was true. If you thought about it, though, it made sense. It occurred to me as I drove through the toll that the man who told me that was probably going to die today, and I clutched the steering wheel, and lit a cigarette, and told myself to shut up, shut up, shut up.

Mike had done a lot for me growing up. His hard work made it so that I didn't have to worry about certain things. He passed on what he knew through experience, he did things with the understanding that This Is The Way It Is Done, and that you would learn from him through careful observation. If he had to show you something, he would point at himself and say, "Watch this." In a way, his teaching was the quietest thing about him, and maybe the only thing you could ever refer to as subtle.

He worked in the belief that for all he did, he might succeed in only moving the world forward just a few inches. His philosophy classes in college had probably contributed to his ability to sum up his little theories on life in succinct phrases. "The first step to happiness is embracing your own worthlessness." He liked that one. He maintained that people thought of themselves as a little too special these days. No one is too important to be replaced anymore, he said. He enjoyed that theme, because it made him seem modest, which he wasn't, and because he firmly believed that in his case, there was no truth to it whatsoever.

As a father, that's what he passed on to you, the ability to show up, to get on with it, and not to get too excited. I thought about this on the way down, how oddly unaffected I felt, how relatively serene I was.

By the time I got to this hospital, I had had it. As I pulled off the Parkway and saw the bright lights of Neptune for the first time, I thought that something had better damn well be happening today for me to come to a place like this. It was that kind of nowhere town in Jersey that feels like a hundred other places. It has an Applebee's somewhere, and a deli called Deli and a pizza place called Mario's owned by some guy named Ahmed, and lots of nice little houses that go on for miles and, most likely, some place called Cheeky's somewhere down near the old railroad tracks.

In all my previous experience, hospitals seemed like airports and shopping malls to me; there was a ton of things happening around you, but you were never sure where to go. I parked and felt certain as I looked up at the massive hospital that I would waste precious minutes looking for them, that they were buried deep in the place in some specialist unit. I walked in the nearest door and standing there, as if we'd planned it, were my mother and two sisters and the requisite boyfriends, talking to some doctors.

It would be nice to say that none of us knew what to say to one another, but the truth was this was the same old thing as the thing before. My sister Gwyneth had been hit by a car and nearly killed at age four. Kathy's brother Mike was run over and killed by a drunk in his twenties. Even for my father Michael, this was his second trip. He had spent eight months in the hospital with acute viral encephalitis, dying slowly, before he just got up one day and got the hell over it. If anyone there knew how familiar this milling around in hospitals waiting for news was to the family, they might have paid us less attention and offered us less coffee.

I wanted to know how he was, but there were too many people looking at all of us. We were clearly Today's Bad News. I noticed that Kathy was wearing a "Life Is Good" T-shirt, before they had become ubiquitous, and I pointed at it and told her it was good that she had prepared for some serious irony today. Everyone kind of laughed. There was no evidence of any tears, no panic, no hysterics. We had pulled it together for now.

The staff took us into a little room and brought in coffee. We sat there, and I got the full story. The guy who hit him was only eighteen, and he had fallen asleep at the wheel. Marty had been hit, too; he'd broken his leg pretty badly. His son had gotten to the scene first. He had known the cop who was first to arrive. Marty's son had come over to the house and woken everyone up and driven them down to the scene.

The details were relayed in voices that should have been shrill and hysterical, given what they were describing. Mike had been struggling with the paramedics when they arrived. The injury to his head was so bad that it was hard for them to believe he was alive, much less able to push back against anything. Kathy had gone to him to calm him down, because he was trying to fight off the EMTs.

What people don't know about brain injuries, what I only found out later, is that the brain does not die right away. It's a slow process. So out there, on the road, his brain was still dying when he fought against the cops and the paramedics. He did not know what was happening to him, he'd never seen or heard the truck, he'd woken up on the road with all of these people around him. When Kathy got there, he stopped fighting, he still recognized her in those moments after impact. She laid him down on the highway, his head shattered and his blood splashed across her shirt, and when she helped hold his head, she asked the paramedics was he going, was he going to go right here on the road? They didn't say anything. They looked at each other and kept working, and there was her answer.

They landed the helicopter at the Mantoloking Yacht Club and took him away, the cop telling Kathy that if they took an ambulance, he died, no question. Marty's son drove them all up to the hospital, and here they had waited for someone to tell them what was going to happen.

Kathy took me aside. "You need to get us a priest. He's dying." It was a Sunday morning. This was a tall order.

"All of the ones we know are pretty far from here. But I'll get him."

"Get one. I don't care how you do it."

I called Dave Edmunds. He had grown up near us at the beach, and when he had become a Marine and then a State Trooper, no one was surprised. The guy was what the Marines liked to call "mission focused." You gave him an objective, and he would tear things apart until he got to it. There was no stopping him. He had a thing for Mike, some sort of hard-ass understanding about everything.

He picked up his phone, and I gave him the story. "I'm on it, man. Sit tight. How long's he got?"

"Maybe not so long."

"I can work with that.".

Exactly thirty-five minutes later, Dave pulled up in an unmarked Crown Victoria, laying rubber all over the parking lot and pulling right up to the door in a squeal of tires. In the passenger seat was a big old priest. He was unhappy.

Dave was wearing shorts, a State Trooper T-shirt, and a firearm. He walked around the car and opened the door, saying only, "Father."

"You people are insane," barked the old padre. He jabbed his finger in my face. "Do you have any idea what it looks like in this day and age for an armed police officer to take you off the altar in front of an entire congregation? Do you? My name is Mud!"

"Thanks for coming."

He looked at the two of us like he was going to damn us all to hell. Dave's expression was the same one he had worn since the day I met him when we were ten years old: I'm here, point me in the right direction.

The priest scowled. "Show me the man."

When the priest was done and gone, the five of us talked some more, everyone wondering what to think. At some point, a woman walked in and said she was part of the Family Team or something like that. We all kind of laughed. "So I guess the news is bad when someone like you comes in?" I said to her. She didn't say anything.

My sister poured her a coffee and said, "Don't worry, lady. Nobody here is going to go to pieces on you." She looked like she really wanted to get out of there. Eventually, she did, leaving the room for saner pastures.

Gwynn and I went out to talk. "I want you to know something," she whispered. "And don't tell Kathy." I nodded.

"If he's not going to be Mike anymore, I don't want him to live. He wouldn't go on like that if it were up to him. So if it's a choice, will you make sure she does the right thing?"

"Have no doubt." We went back inside.

A few doctors came in and out, and we spoke to them. Mike was stable and they were doing what they needed before they got him upstairs.

One of them asked me, "Do you want to see him?"

"I can see him?"

"Yes."

"Do I want to see him?"

He shrugged a bit and motioned me into one of the rooms, and there was Mike. I had pictured a team of doctors surrounding him, pushing things into him, doing something, anyway. But there was just the one doctor, in hospital greens, standing over him like a sentinel.

He was lying down, and to me, he looked dead. There was blood on his head and on his hands, and they had put some kind of white cloth around his lower half. He didn't move, he barely breathed. I wondered, was this goodbye time? Or were they just letting me see him for some other reason? The doctor and I looked at each other.

"Can he hear me?"

"Probably not." To hell with this guy. I stood over Mike. He was motionless. A thought that ran through my head then would keep coming to me in the coming months: here he is, the great man, laid low. You always wonder what you'll say when things come down to it. What would be the one thing you'd say if you might never see someone ever again? You'd say anything you'd think they'd want to hear right then.

"We're all here, Mike." I touched his hand, and squeezed it. Nothing moved. It didn't even feel like a hand anymore to me. "Sit tight. I'll take care of this."

The rest of the day passed in a rush of faces. People came from all over that Sunday, just to be there. They would keep coming for weeks, and you were glad for it, glad to just have them sit there, even if all you were going to do was stare at one another. It was enough to just have someone to look at and ask if they could believe just how bad this all was.

My mother's brother had been killed by a car when he was twenty-four. The shape he ended up in, there had been no question about which way things were going to go. He was just a kid, still drinking all night and coming over to our house and cleaning out any booze that wasn't hidden under the floorboards. Mike Nolan loved him for reasons no one ever really grasped. The hospital had kept him alive until everyone had gotten there, and then they all went in and said goodbye. You wouldn't think it, but Mike was the last person in there in that hospital room, looking at Kathy's dying baby brother. You didn't think a guy like that would even stick around, but there he was, shaking his head. I asked him once what he had been thinking there, the last man in the room, and for once, he had an answer. "It was a waste of a good kid. People hate that."

They brought us in to see Mike when they had gotten him settled, and that first sight was when it really came down. He was in a bed with tubes and wires pouring out of him. His head was bandaged; they had covered up the worst of it. When I saw that, I knew there was no way he was walking out of there. If he didn't die there, he was still going to die sometime soon. There was nothing you could do for someone in his shape.

I tried to think of human things to do in a situation like this. I put my hand on Kathleen's shoulder. I thought of what my sister had said outside the doors of the hospital, and now standing there looking down at him, helpless and strapped in, waiting to die in a building full of strangers, I wanted him to die. If he was going to go, let him go now, with us in the room, not after weeks or months of hanging on, his life dripping out of him through all of these machines. He still looked strong; let him go out strong, let him go out having given it a good fight, to have not died on the road, to have hung on until the helicopter and the cops got him to the hospital, so we could all be there by his side to watch him go.

I was sure it was what he would have asked of me. Let his mother see him, and then let him go. Give the guy his dignity. That's what I wanted for him too, not to die in front of all of these people.

We all talked to him, people saying what was important. The five of us stood there, each taking turns, talking about how he was going to make it through this one. I called him "Buddy" and "Pal" and told him he was my man. When we got to my sister Gwynn, we all got very quiet. She was a lawyer, too. Maybe she could lay some of that smooth lawyer talk on him, bring him back into the boardroom, make him feel at home.

"Awww, Dad, yeeeeaaaaah, it's ooooookaaaaaaay, yeeeeaaaaaaah. Alright, Daddy, it's aaaaaaaalllllll ooooooookaaaaaaay, yeeeeeaaaaaaah."

I looked up at Kathleen and Michaela. Kathleen turned to her. "Hey, are you trying to make the guy throw up in his feeding tube? Shut the fuck up."

The nurse in the corner snorted involuntarily and left the room. Everyone else but Mike laughed.

They told us to all go home eventually. There would be nothing new tonight.

"Will he die today?"

"Probably not."

"Tomorrow?"

"Maybe."

"So we're not out of the woods?"

"No."

Looking around the room, you could see all the faces saying, "Don't make us leave him."

That night I drove Kathleen home, the girls following behind us in her car. I figured she would cry when it was time to leave Mike there that first night in the hospital by himself, but she didn't. She tugged at my sleeve when it was time to go, and we walked out, a crowd of about thirty of us.

I played songs for her the whole way back, and it would become a bit of a ritual between us, me driving her home for days after it happened, playing her these songs she'd never heard, telling her it would all be cool and knowing it would not be.

When we got home, I poured us two huge vodka tonics. We talked that night, out on the beach, not like a mother and a son, but like two old friends. She told me that she loved him more than anyone else in the world, and how she felt that made her special, to be able to love a man even his own mother didn't love. The nerve of that asshole, she said, to go and die on her this way.

When I was fourteen, I broke a bunch of vertebrae playing lacrosse. When I came home, the old man, who was never at home, was waiting in my room, the place where I would spend an entire summer on my back, staring at the walls and demanding something to read until I healed. Everything hurt; it hurt to move a finger. He came in and sat on the other bed in his evaluation mode. He looked at me lying there and all he said was, "Well?"

I told him this sucked, it would be a summer wasted, no sports, no beach, no friends, no nothing. The doctor had told me that my days of running around beating on people with a stick in my hand were over, I would never play again, it would be too dangerous.

"Easy now, hero," Mike said. "It wasn't like you were going to college based upon your skills on the field. You'll need to get better if you're going to get out there again, though. You want to get out there again, right?'

I did want to get out there again. "Don't listen to those doctors, they're all quacks," he said. "They're a bunch of nancies. You can take a hit. Here, I want you to have this." From around his neck he took off a silver chain with a medal shaped like a cross hanging from it. "St. Christopher Medal. Your Uncle Eddie gave this to me a long time ago, when he thought I was going to Vietnam. It kept him safe through five years of the war . . ." The Legend of Eddie, his uncle, who in the family telling had fought through every major battle of the war in Europe. We all knew it by heart.

I took it in my hands. "Five years without a scratch," he said, walking to the windows and looking out on Ocean Terrace.

". . . ten different countries . . ."

". . . a thousand dead Nazis . . ."

". . . killing with his bare hands . . ."

". . . blood up to his boots . . ."

". . . a chestful of medals . . ."

"And this is the one that counted. It's yours, pal. You wear that, and you can go back to playing. Not a scratch on you."

The medal was beat up and had turned dark. I twisted it in my hand and turned it over. "I Am A Catholic, Please Call A Priest," it read.

That night in the hospital, I had tucked St. Christopher into the small bag of Mike's stuff we were allowed to leave in a drawer next to his bed. In the blue flickering light of all the machines, I could see his face beneath the bandages, sleeping now, maybe for good.

"It's yours again, buddy. If you ever wake up, you put this on. See you tomorrow."

Chapter 5

PUZZLES LIKE YOU

Was I ever just a normal guy? I mean, did we ever just do regular
    father and son stuff?
Sure we did. We met up for haircuts and lunch every month.
That's it?
Well, there were the holidays.
Christ.

Mike and I never talked much and we never talked about things between him and his old man. It wasn't that I'd ever brought it up and
been told not to. It was just that Mike let you know there were things
he didn't ever want to talk about. He could make his silence on a topic
seem like something physical. To raise the issue would be to invite his
hard stare, a window into his serenely boiling rage, always lurking,
always behind his glasses and his icy blue eyes. His mouth might curl,
his hands clench, his face redden. What came after would be volcanic,
horrible and unforgettable. If you'd seen it once, you never wanted to
see it again.

But we did have things between us that kept us together. Every
three weeks, since I was two years old, we got our hair cut together, always at the same place. He first took me there after an incident that has
since become notorious in our house, something everyone can laugh
about now, but only with the passing of three decades. I had blonde
hair when I was a kid, and my Mom loved it, and she would never cut
it. One day my old man and I were at the liquor store and some lady

mentioned to him what a cute little girl he had, on account of my long blonde hair. She might as well have kneed him in the balls.

That was it. He left the shopping cart in the aisle with the booze in it and drove straight to the shop, where they cut it all off. Mom cried when she saw me, and Mike lamely handed her a little baggy of my blonde locks as a peace offering. He would know no peace for weeks on account of this little stunt.

Everyone who went to the place referred to it only as "The Shop." It looked like a regular house from the outside, only the entire downstairs was the business with wall to ceiling mirrors in one room where you got your hair cut and a waiting area which was like a living room with couches and a TV.

Everyone went there, from politicians to lawyers to mobsters to you name it, but it was only for men. There was always food lying around, and coffee made and a full bar. Guys came in who weren't getting their hair cut at all. Guys came in who were bald—it didn't matter. You'd go in and everyone would be talking at each other, what passed for yelling in Irish households. But for Italians, this was just communication. I'd sit silently and watch them, shouting and waving their arms around and saying "Ahhhh" to one another dismissively, all the time switching between Italian and English. They'd get so animated, you were sure there was going to be a fight, and then they'd be laughing and calling each other names. There was so much emotion and energy, I got tired just watching them. In our family, if someone raised their voice and waved their hands, it meant someone was about to break someone else's nose.

You walked in: "Heeeeeeeeeeeeeeeeeeeey, Michael! Heeeeeeeeeeeeeeeeeey, Sean! OK!!! How's it going?! All right!" It wasn't said in a tough guy way, it was said in a way that made you feel like you were there to see a couple of uncles you hadn't seen in forever but that you always loved growing up.

They were three brothers. Cosmo and Jerry spoke perfect English, but the third brother Mike never learned. He was always quiet. So quiet you wondered why he ever bothered learning Italian, because he never used that either. They all wore suits and ties when they cut hair. What Mike would call a "classy place." The only thing that said class to the old man more than an accent was a suit and tie. They would speak Italian to one another, and I always had this vague but persistent worry that they were talking about us. What if, even though they professed to like us, they harbored secret loathing and were saying things like, "Look at this pale, freckley little shit, ahhh? I'd like to cut his fucking ears off." You'd never know until they were gone.

When I was a kid, Mike used to tell me to sit still when Cosmo cut my hair, because he had a collection of bad little boys' ears in the back. If you squirmed, he just might take them off. This did nothing to allay my fears that perhaps there was an Italian plot to make me the secret ingredient in a big pot of sauce that was probably boiling somewhere in the back. Cosmo was fast with the scissors, and these guys were always talking and moving their arms and spinning around to call another guy a jerk or ask did he know what the hell he was talking about. I was concerned he would miss my hair one day and scalp me by accident.

They also had dirty magazines there, mostly just old *Playboys*—they were mixed in along with all the *Business Week*s, and I would pretend to be seriously rifling through *National Geographic*s and *Guns & Ammo*s, all the while hunting for the good stuff. Mike would be talking to the guys, and I'd be back there, checking them out. The guys coming back to use the can would never say anything, other than maybe, "Get a good look, kiddo."

The air would be smoky and filled with the smell of booze and coffee and swishy hair products and hair dryers. And always yelling. Occasionally, Cosmo would break it up with a piece of song sung with no tune whatsoever. He spoke the song; he didn't sing it. It was delivered in monotone, albeit with an Italian accent, so to the American ear, it sounded fantastic. And he would add his own lyrics: "Uptown girl . . . you are living in your uptown world . . . backstreet guuuuuy . . . you fucking bitch . . . you don't take my call . . ."

The guys spoke in exclamation points. Every sentence was a statement, delivered as loudly as possible and sprinkled with massive profanity. Everybody was yelling at everybody else or pretending to have no goddamn idea what the other guy was talking about. The talk was constant. There were never any quiet moments. Feigned confusion went over well with this crowd. From the second you walked in to the second you left, it sounded like somebody standing next to you banging a gong.

"Joey, where's that place? The Blue Iguana or what the fuck is it?"

"The blue what? The blue who?" Joey would give an exasperated look to the guy and shrug his shoulders at everyone else: *this guy is crazy, what can I do?*

"Come on, me and you and Cos and Mike were there for New Years, the place with the palm trees."

"You're fucked up with palm trees. I wouldn't go to a place like that."

"You believe this guy? Do you believe this fucking guy? YOU, and ME, and fucking COS, we were all THERE, for fucking Newyearseve."

Cos would chime in, "Yeah, I know it, you know it, Joey, what is it—the blue something, the Blue Ape?"

Now would commence the waving of arms and the swearing— Cos had said something stupid. "Ahhhhh, you fucking ape, fucking ape, what the fuck." This went on the whole time you were there— insane conversations with no beginning and no end. Really, it was the same conversation, continuing for decades. It all boiled down to remembering the one place in New York/Las Vegas/Portofino/Paris where you ate/danced/drank/screwed so you could tell another guy where to do all the same stuff.

I would sit there soaking it all in, watching the back and forth and speaking only when spoken to. If I was ever addressed, it would usually consist of, "Sean, you believe this guy? Come on!" I would nod or shrug my shoulders. These guys were conversational heavyweights, and I knew I wasn't yet in their league.

Mike would join in regularly, but since he wasn't big on talking about drinking or screwing, he would usually talk about the latest great restaurant he'd been to in the city with a client. The guys in the shop went nuts for this kind of thing. If they weren't eating, they were talking about where they just ate or where they would be eating that night. If Mike liked a place, it was "TREH-men-dous." If it wasn't so great, it was, "Give it a pass." The guys would all nod to one another, as Mike Nolan was reputed to know his restaurants. If it was especially good, he would make a pistol with his hand and point it at the mirror in front of him. "Classy place."

When we were done, they'd wheel you around in the chair and hold a mirror to the back of your head so you could see it. I didn't even know what to look for, but I always told Cos it was a masterpiece. "OK, a—SEAN!" he'd say, and you jumped off the chair. Mike would be up at the counter paying Jerry, and he'd slip him back the tip, and Jerry would say thank you, and then Mike would slyly hand me five dollars to give to Cosmo. I'd go over and try to do it the way the other guys did it—palm the bill and shake hands so that it stayed in their fist. I never could quite do it, and when I raised it with Mike, he said, "Don't worry about that, it means you're honest."

We would leave to a chorus of "Ciao's"—"Ciao, Mike! Ciao, Sean! Ciao! Ciao!" All my life, the only two places that have ever been the same, no matter where I was and where I came back from, were the shop and the beach, and I missed both whenever I was away for too long.

Once it changed, but only once. One day we went to the shop and Mike, the third brother, the quiet one, was gone. I asked Jerry where he was and he said, "He left. He said something about me and Cos always talking in English around here; he thought we were always talking about him. What the fuck is that?"

We planned our haircuts around going to Pal's Cabin. Pal's was a place popular with the same type of people who frequented The Shop. There were a lot of guys in suits, and you could never really tell which side of the law they were on. There were older couples who looked like they came there every day and had probably been doing so for fifty years. In some ways, it seemed like another kind of club. There was a sameness to the people in there; they were the kind of people who would come out for lunch at a place where the menu had not changed in decades, and who would never want it to.

We always went there after The Shop, and we always ordered the same thing—two chocolate shakes, two bowls of mushroom soup with the bread basket and two cheeseburger platters, with bacon. Mike always ordered. It got to the point where they didn't give us menus anymore, and the waitresses stopped asking us what we wanted, which was a good thing, because the waitresses were all pretty crazy. Most of them had blue hair and argued with you about what you really wanted to eat and whether you could make any changes to what was on the menu. "Ya got that last time, mix it up, guys. For the love." They hated you, but no one seemed to mind.

The tenor of these meetings between Mike and I never seemed to change, no matter how much older I got. They basically came down to the old man asking how I was doing in school and then work and where I was with my life plan. He had always had a plan. He called it "self-actualizing." He had learned this in college, he told me. You had to decide what you wanted to be, and then do everything to be that thing. So he would say, "What do you want to be?" and I wouldn't know and it would start like that.

"Well, what would you like to be?"

"I'm not too sure."

"Everybody wants to be something."

"OK, I want to be a lawyer."

"Why?"

"I dunno. You and Grandpa are lawyers, and it seems like something I could do."

"You don't want to be a lawyer."

"Why not?"

"Trust me. You don't." All lawyers say this.

"OK."

"So what do you want to be?"

The circle would go around and around like this, until, at last, I would confess to just having no clue what I wanted to be. Then he would get to say his line.

"You're not self-actualizing."

"No?"

"No."

"Oh."

He lived for this. He loved being self-actualizing. Whenever Mike heard something or learned something that didn't have anything to do with the law, he remembered about one percent of it, and he would repeat that one percent as often as he could. I firmly believe that in four years as a philosophy major, this represented the sum total of what he'd absorbed. Self-actualization. It made him feel good. It made him feel like the law wasn't everything he knew and liked, as if he dabbled in philosophy in his spare time.

Once, Joe took me to get my hair cut at his guy, some guy named Angelo in Bayhead. The guy was Italian, and he had a nice shop. He and Joe talked about everything, the same stuff that the guys back at the shop talked about. Only it wasn't the same. He tried to talk to me while he cut my hair, like Cosmo always did, but I didn't want to talk. I was annoyed. He was a fraud as far as I was concerned. There was the shop, there was Cosmo, there was Jerry, there were the guys sitting around smoking, and that was the real thing. This? It felt like a con.

Joe and I even went out for burgers after, just like Mike and I did. That felt wrong, too. We sat on some deck looking out over the bay on a gorgeous afternoon, but it wasn't the same. I would have rather been sitting at Pal's drinking a chocolate milkshake and looking out at the Exxon station on Mt. Prospect Avenue. As much as I loved spending any time I could with Joe, there were things that were just for Mike and me, even if he did ask me about my life plan and try to find out whether I'd become self-actualizing or not.

Mike would move off of philosophy and gradually start talking about other things. He hated most people. You could tell because he used to say things like, "I hate most people." He honestly thought that most of the world was lazy, fat or stupid, and probably all three. You could tell when he met someone, he was always sizing them up to see if they were lazy or stupid—obesity would be evident already. But he suspected much of the world was susceptible to all three, including us.

He knew we weren't stupid, but he was always worried about you getting fat or lazy. At dinner, it was pointless to take seconds of anything. He'd spend the whole time staring at you, like you might suddenly explode into a giant lard-ass right in front of him. He'd watch you eating, and in the end it wasn't worth it. God help you if you were watching TV around him, ever. He was at work most nights and weekends, but he would occasionally be home, and if he caught you in front of the TV, you were finished. He'd give you something to do right away, like cleaning the garage. He liked movement and progress.

Mike and I would sit there in Pal's, having lunch or dinner, and we'd talk about what I should do, and occasionally he'd tell me what he was doing. But a long time after we stopped going, I realized that in all the hundreds of times I'd met him there, I never once had a conversation about him. I couldn't tell you his politics or his religion or his favorite color. Nobody could. He didn't have those things.

For him, there was always the law, and his relationship to it was different than his father's. His father became a lawyer because it was a way to make some money, and he genuinely liked it and he liked the people that came with it. His friends were cops and firemen and lawyers and judges and he hung out with them, and they all got along. He did it because he loved it, but it didn't own him. The money, the stuff, the friends—they were all icing. He would have done it anyway.

Mike Nolan's core motivation in all things was winning. At any given moment, you could be sure that his head was mulling over one thing: how to beat someone, anyone, at anything. He chose the field in life where he knew he had the best chance of winning. He became a lawyer because he had to.

A lot of that competitiveness must have come from things with his old man. I always saw him taking note of the cars and the houses and the friends, because he had to have more than Joe if he wanted to be declared the winner. He didn't love any of it, he didn't enjoy any of it. He didn't buy the house to have the house to make himself or his family happy. He did it because it was part of the game, another chip, another step closer to victory. You could see the outlines of his plan in the way he had shaped his life—become a lawyer, emulate his father, only do it better, work that much longer and harder at everything than Joe or anyone else did. He would be there for his clients when they called, like his old man. He would come to hospitals and funerals and wrecked cars by the side of the road, just like his old man. But he could never pull that part off.

He just didn't have that. He had friends—maybe two or three. Guys he'd known all his life. He didn't trust anyone else.

Clients loved Joe and hired him because he was a friend and he happened to be a great lawyer. They hired Mike because he was a great lawyer who went through the motions of being a friend. Sure, he'd go to the weddings and wakes and funerals and dinner parties, but he didn't really want to be there. You could tell. Everyone knew. He was rude, he was dismissive, he said nasty things and made sure you knew he wasn't kidding, even though he'd say he was.

Wherever he was, he wanted to be back at the office. Work was the only thing that truly made him happy in life, besides my mother and the kids. And even with us, you got the feeling that we made him happy because we accepted that he would only be happy at the office. We let him go and work and didn't complain about it.

You meet guys sometimes who say things like, "my old man was never around, he worked so hard," like it's a boo-hoo type of thing. You want to tell them to go and fuck themselves, because who did you think he was busting his ass for all goddamn day? I never felt bad about Mike working, not one bit. He was miserable when he was home anyway, and everyone was happy doing their own thing. I can't see the reason in getting everyone upset just so we could pretend to want each other around.

He was a guy you could never figure out whether to hate, fear or feel bad for. We'd sit there, and he'd even eat in an angry way, attacking the burger, first by slicing the poor thing in half—overhand, so it was like he was stabbing it. Then he'd just destroy the thing. There would be pieces of it all over the plate, and he'd stab at them and the French fries with his fork, each time hitting them so hard that the fork would go right through the food and hit the plate.

Still, I loved watching him just live. He was in motion, constant motion. When I was seven years old he took me on a visit to a car manufacturing plant he represented because I was obsessed with *Star Wars* and robots. I remember giant machines moving back and forth in a never-ending ballet of progress, churning cars past them, sending sparks flying up into the air. He and I stood there in hard hats, both of us mesmerized at the choreography but for very different reasons.

I thought of Mike in that factory. Like those machines, he would never stop. None of this would ever end for him, although he talked about the end, constantly. He would retire, he said, and run his charity, Kids Corporation, full time. He and Mom would go on vacations, and he would never answer the phone or send another letter or wear a tie again. But he talked about it like a condemned man talking to his family about how he'd be seeing them real soon the night before the big hanging in the village square. You all knew it wasn't true. None of that was ever going to happen, but it was nice to know he thought it was worth saying it anyway. He was hip to the fact that real people looked forward to things like that.

We'd sit and he'd talk about some hump at work who was trying to screw him. Or how he'd gotten someone, real good. He loved to get people. He had an expression I heard him use a few times on the phone to people who had crossed him. "It's a small world. You and I are going to meet again." Click.

The man had a lot of loathing for a lot of people. They were an annoyance for him, a speed bump on the road to victory, with their questions and qualifiers and their shades of gray. He would look out the window and talk about them, how stupid they were, how "their shit" was costing him money. When he talked, you hated them, too. You couldn't help it. He was moving, always. And it is beautiful to see a machine do what it was built to do. He could never stop and you wouldn't want him to. The running gave him meaning. Without it, he was just another fat, lazy, stupid person eating a burger in New Jersey.

He'd be eating and sucking down a Diet Coke, and you could feel his restless energy singing to you, "Don't you know I have to go?" He always had to go. It was always something. It didn't matter if you were still eating. He'd hand the waitress the credit card, and he'd already have his jacket on and be looking at his watch.

"Ready to go, man?"

Chapter 6

THE TIGERS HAVE SPOKEN

I think I must be something like my father. I don't know him anymore, but I think that what I am . . . it must be something like him. There have to be so many things I learned about being myself, being a lawyer. He must be a lot like me.

In a lot of ways he is, and in a few others, not so much.

No? Well. That's sad. Are you anything like me?

I'm more like you than I let on for a long time. I'm a lot like you, I just make it look a whole lot better than you ever did.

So what did I teach you?

Shitloads. You taught a lot of people a lot of things about How Things Really Are.

The old man had a way of sneaking up on people, especially when they didn't do their homework. He liked to think the world underestimated him, like he was always the snake in the long grass, lying in wait for the big payback. In my last year of college, I took a class called American Justice, thinking there was still a part of me that wanted to go to law school and that maybe the law involved justice. It was taught by a woman who was more than sure it did. This lady bled green for the planet. She knew that arms were for hugging, not for war. And she knew that war was bad for children and other living things. Mike would have called her "one of them," and you knew what he meant.

Believers.

Idealists.

Fantasists.

Hippies.

Shitheads.

The thing is, she was more than the bumper-stickered VW ex-hippie bore that people took her for at first. Sure, she railed on about a lot of that stuff, the Earth and war and corporations and finding yourself and all that Sixties bullshit, but she was a decent person.

She meant what she said, and the cool thing about her was that she wasn't bitter or vitriolic about it. She knew that most of the kids in her classes came from well-off whitey-type places, and maybe she had a shot at making you think about everyone else for a bit before you went off and made more than your parents ever did. Basically, she was a very good person who wanted you to be one, too.

All of which made her eventual meeting with J. Michael Nolan, Jr., probably the worst day of her life.

The class consisted of a lot of reading about various actual events, most having to do with some corporation screwing the little guy. Or it was the government abusing someone or trampling on their rights. I got the picture, and I was with her on most of it. Nobody likes a bully, and I'd been there. So OK, I was into it.

She had come up to me after class and asked if my father was the same Mike Nolan who came in to speak at the law school a few times a semester.

"Yes, that's him."

"He frequently writes about environmental law," she said.

"Oh yeah?" She looked at me like I had an orange growing out of my forehead. "Oh. Yeah."

"He runs a charity, doesn't he? To educate kids in Newark?"

"He does. Kids Corporation."

"I hear they do great work, and he sounds like someone who could teach the kids here a lot about being successful and giving back to the country at the same time."

"He's not exactly how he looks on paper, I just want you to know that," I said.

"Well, think he would be interested in speaking to the class?"

"Sure, I could ask him."

"I think people would really appreciate someone who has been there and seen all the ups and downs of really being in the trenches, fighting the fight."

"You've read his papers?"

"Oh, yes."

"All of them? All the way through?" I was waiting for her to let me in on the joke.

"All the way through. Let me know what he says."

My friend JP was going to law school the following year and was familiar with the man, having been woken up by him on several occasions when my folks had come to visit, standing over his bed and asking when we nancies were going to get up and start partying like men. As we walked out of class, he laughed in my face. "Ohhhh, man. This is going to be terrible for you. Mike Nolan. She is going to get what she paid for."

The appointed day for Mike to speak to my class arrived faster than I would have liked. When he was visiting me at school in Indiana, thousands of miles from anything like an ocean, he would take me to lunch at a fish restaurant, because he thought it was funny. This was the kind of thing he really enjoyed, taking you to the only place in town worse than the dining hall.

"Oh shit, that is goooooooood," he'd say, getting himself into some disgusting fish burger whose contents had last seen the ocean a week ago, if he was lucky.

I was now old enough to not respond. I'd just sort of look at him and then look out the window facing onto the St. Joseph's River, the one bone this place had thrown their customers—at least it was near some water.

The old man messed with everybody, but he was one of those guys for whom the phrase "Better to have him pissing out than pissing in," was written for. People would hire him just so he wouldn't be on the other side. If he was your guy, that was it, he was your shark, your personal pitbull, the nightmare you inflicted on others. He was happy to be all of those things. He reveled in the hatred and disgust people sometimes threw his way.

"Do me a favor today?"

"Sure."

"Go easy on the whole being yourself thing."

He feigned shock and insult. "Why? What's so wrong with me?"

"You know how these kinds of people react to you."

"You mean ivory tower potheads?"

"Normal people. People not like us. They're into things, they care about people and animals and the Earth and shit. They're into organizations and going to meetings."

"They can go to hell. I do more good for more people when I'm not even on the clock than they do crying about goddamn whales all day."

"So you'll take it easy?"

"Sure."

There were simple ways to provoke him. You could do things like question his judgment, or tell him his tie looked like hell, or that he didn't work all that hard. That type of thing would earn you a biting putdown, usually along the lines of a comparison between your relevance in the world and a piece of dogshit he'd stepped on a week ago. You didn't have to waste much time speculating on which one meant more to him.

Or you could ask him to take it easy.

He arrived in true Mike Nolan fashion, a perfectly timed three minutes late so the audience would be quiet and notice his entrance. The professor had already begun talking about today's guest speaker, a corporate lawyer from New York who would give us an inside look on the various nefarious machinations of corporate America. JP giggled next to me like a schoolgirl, shaking his head and high-fiving our friends around us. I kept my head down.

Mike looked every inch the part in his sharkskin suit, blue tie and bullshit Italian loafers. He bounced purposefully down the stairs, surveying the class slowly, like I'd seen him look at the members of a jury, sizing up so many people in so many seconds. Stock taken, he smiled and put his hand out to the professor. She shook it.

"So here we have Mike Nolan, father of Sean Nolan. He lectures here in our law school, and he's agreed to speak to us today about what he does and how the white collar criminal world he works in pertains to our studies here."

Mike stood silently for a few seconds, looking out at the hundred or so kids in the room. Finally, he began in a voice as clear and authoritative as a drill sergeant. "Write down everything I say." There was a rustling of paper and some skeptical looks between the audience.

"Thanks for having me. I have three things to tell you today, and they are as follows: One, do not trust the government. I know, I used to work for them. Two, you will not save the world on your own, and most of it is not worth saving anyhow. Keep your goals realistic and stay focused on what you want. Three, realize your own worthlessness. Don't think too much of yourself. I've seen enough college graduates to know what they're worth. Trust me on all points, and try not to be insulted."

A few kids looked around like someone had crapped their pants next to them.

"Point one, the government. They are not your friends. Sure, they do nice things, they send you a check when you're old, and if you're lucky, some day a cop or a firefighter might save your life. But that's not what I mean. I'm talking about the real government, the faceless bureaucrats who can decide to deprive you of your livelihood and freedom whenever they want.

"I assume you all enrolled in this class because you were interested in justice. That's good, you should be. You should hope that there is justice out there. You should hope that the law treats you with fairness and that those enforcing it are restrained in its application and more interested in truth than retribution. You should hope that you never do anything or are unlucky enough to draw their attention." He had them already, in those first few seconds. There was absolute silence, and all eyes were on him.

"That said, hope is for suckers and socialists. Don't fool yourself, ever. If all those fairy tales were true, there wouldn't be people like me. And as much as what I will tell you in the next hour may repulse and offend you, I assure you that every word of it is true. Listen to what I have to say, I know what I'm talking about. Some people take years in jail or millions of dollars or both before they understand what I'm telling you. And here you are, getting it for free." Mike gave examples of people he'd defended who were messed with by the government for one reason or another, and who, of course, thanks to him, were proved totally and absolutely innocent and without blame. He stood there like Captain America after each story, as if to say, "Goddamn, I am good. Are you all picking up on that?"

The class was hooked. He looked the part, he sounded the part, he could have been the slick big city lawyer in any number of TV dramas. It was clear that he meant what he said and knew what he was talking about, and even kids our age were smart enough to know that wasn't always so common in the halls of academia. This man wasn't interested in mincing any words. He had been to the courthouse and knew the score.

I'd seen him appear in front of the New Jersey Supreme Court once. He walked in like a king, not looking at anyone in the gallery, looking only straight ahead. You could tell he was among his people there, that walking down the street he could have been any well-dressed lawyer, but here, people respected what he'd done and what he was. Seeing him in his world made me understand a bit why he and his father loved it so much. Most of the time, it just seemed like a drag. Today it seemed like excellent television.

"Point two, your mission in life. A lot of kids your age embrace all kinds of happy horseshit. You know the ones: they've got Amnesty International stickers on their windows. Guess what? That sticker doesn't free any political prisoners. They're vegetarians. McDonald's just served their billionth customer. The point is, who cares? Believing in something doesn't mean shit.

"You want to care about something? Do something. Lose the stickers and stop going to marches. No one gives a shit, and it doesn't change anything, trust me. I was around for Vietnam, so I remember back when people your age had real problems. You want to make a difference to real people? Go to work teaching in a city during the summer, do something that gives of your time and your fancy-pants education here at this university. A letter to the school newspaper doesn't mean you changed anything; it just means you can read and write, and they're not exactly handing out awards for that anymore.

"Most of all, realize this. We are all just moving things forward a little bit at a time. Chances are you will not be Jesus, or Gandhi or Abraham Lincoln. You will probably just get a job at some company making some widget, and when you're dead, no one will really remember you. That's a fact. But don't let it get you down. You can still do your part. Moving the chains forward is all that matters, if at the end of everything you moved them even an inch in the right direction, you will have counted for something.

"You will never make any difference if you spread yourself too thin, so pick something and get to it. Know how to tell someone who doesn't mean shit to the world and isn't moving the chains forward? They're driving a Volvo with a hundred stickers on it about how war is bad and whales are good and children are great. That means they lack focus, they care about everything so they do nothing." He dragged out that last word for about three seconds.

Then, he turned to the front row and pointed at some guy. "Ask me what I care about."

"Uh, what do you care about?"

"None of your damn business, kid. Figure out your own problems. I can't do everything for you, and I don't have a check with your signature on it.

"There are more bad people than good people in the world. A lot more. And whether you're bad or you're good, you get a lawyer. And if you're lucky, you get someone like me. I work for some bad people;

I'm sure all the hippies out throwing hacky sacks in the quad would choke on their bongs if they heard the names. Oil companies. Drug companies. Arms dealers. Some of these people make me sick to be in a room with them, but they deserve me, so they get me.

"How? Simple. I do not care about the whales. Know what that means? It means I don't give a shit about whales. Animals belong in two places: jungles and zoos. I've never seen a whale, although I think it's great that somewhere out there, there are whales. Whales are not what I have chosen to care about. See what I mean? I am effective because I am focused. Be focused. Realize your limits. You can't do it all.

"Finally, point three. You're all pretty special kids if you're here, aren't you? I mean, to be able to come to a place like this, you were probably something else, probably at the top of your class in high school, good at sports, mommy and daddy had some cash, right? For the most part, you are the top of the top, and everyone has probably let you know it. That's the thing now, every kid is special and precious, and the sun shines right out of your asses.

"I hope it does. Just in case it doesn't, be aware of something. There are millions like you. Chances are, you are not special. Some of you have already peaked, getting into this school will be the last thing you ever do of any real consequence. Try not to make that be the case, the world needs strivers. But realize and embrace your own probable worthlessness. It'll make you a better person.

"Someday, if any of you make something of yourselves, chances are, you'll need someone like me. I know I'm not pretty, and I'm not that fun to be around, and most people hate the very idea that people like me are needed in the world. That's OK for two reasons: I don't care what anyone else thinks, and because I am needed. In some small way, some people need me some of the time. Maybe someday that'll be you. Be needed. It's a great feeling, and none of the thousands of assholes you will encounter in your future working lives will be able to justify getting rid of you.

"Try to remember something when they let you out of here. For the first twenty years afterwards, you won't know a goddamn thing. People always forget that. I know I did. Keep your mouth shut and listen to people who know what they're talking about. You could bring that twenty years down to nineteen if you really work at it."

He rapped his knuckles on a desk and smiled his big sarcastic smile. *Chew on that, people.*

"OK. That's it. You can stop writing. I'm done."

The professor had a look on her face like a clown riding a giant monkey had just bolted across the room, something between, "Did that happen?" and "Oh, mother of shit." Mike shook her hand and buttoned his jacket in one motion, and with that, he walked up the stairs and out of the room.

The room broke out into a fury of whispered reviews, and as class was dismissed, I stayed in my seat to face my professor. JP got up and, before leaving, did his best Mike Nolan impersonation, pretending to straighten his tie and standing at attention. "Sean, write this down. Three things. One, your grade point average just ended up in the shitter. Two, your old man's invitation as commencement speaker will definitely not be in the mail. Three, may God have mercy on you and your family."

I sat at my desk, and she walked up the aisle shaking her head. I smiled and tried to act like I was in on some kind of joke here. She did, too.

"So, does he really have that charity and do all those great things for kids?"

"He does."

"He didn't mention it."

"He does not care about the whales."

She sat down, looking across the empty classroom. "Relax. The world needs people like him, too. Otherwise, Volvo-driving liberals like me would be out of a job."

"Thanks."

As I turned to leave, she called out to me. "It's kind of an act, right? I mean, he's not always like that?"

Chapter 7

MY TIME HAS COME

Mike, you were the toughest guy I knew.

I like that. Not tough enough lately. Not tougher than a truck.

I did not actually know you weren't until recently. That's how goddamn
tough you were.

There were few things my mother could say to me after school that
were worse than, "Go outside and play with your friends." A lot of
kids I went to school with could not wait to get home so they could
run out to the park and throw some sort of ball around. Walking down
the big steps of Our Lady of the Lake when school let out, there would
be a cascade of small children running across Bloomfield Avenue to
"go play."

This was normal, and I could see why they liked it, but it was
never for me. I have no doubt their parents assumed that little Timmy
and Joey were throwing the old pigskin around, or playing an innocent game of dodgeball. They would probably look back on rose-tinted
memories of their days in that very same park, playing on the swings,
running across the big fields, maybe some Hide and Go Seek. I am
sure those days existed somewhere, but not when I was a kid.

No, in the late 1970s, there was one game to rule them all in my
town, and that game was known as Smear the Queer or, more accu-
rately, Kill the Man with the Ball. These delightful titles should leave
absolutely no question in anyone's mind as to why a kid with bad hearing and bad eyesight who was at least a foot too small for his age would

not be tearing down the door to get out there and mix it up with the other young fellas in town.

The rules of the game were as simple as the name suggests: whoever picked up the ball, which could be any ball really, but was usually a football, was instantly set upon by EVERY OTHER KID IN THE GAME. That was pretty much the only rule. Pick up the ball, try to advance it somewhat towards the goal before twenty other kids knocked the ever-living shit out of you.

Children are pretty durable, and we knew it. You could take some big shots and go sprawling onto the ground and pop right back up again. Depending on who you played with, the game could actually be fun. But there was always a certain element who found a way to make the game less about good-natured shoving and more about driving your head into the ground and stomping on it.

The element on my street was named Paul. His last name is lost to me, although it could just as easily have been Evil. Paul Evil and the Evil Family lived around the corner from us, and he was just a Bad Kid. Most of the trouble in the neighborhood came from this kid. Smashed pumpkins? Paul. Stolen bike? Paul. Kid with bloody nose? Paul.

He looked the part, too. He had those bizarre fangs that some people just seem to grow, and burning blue eyes and a mouth that never smiled. His hair was a blond rabble on his head, and his ears were almost pointy. His nose perpetually leaked snot. His lip curled over his teeth, like a dog's. I hated his guts.

To get home from school, I had to follow home our next-door neighbors, who were collectively and always known as the Lally Kids. Kathy demanded it. Between school and home, there was a big park which worried my mother to no end. She was afraid of perverts long before it was fashionable, and it didn't help that there were water traps involved. The park was dominated by two huge ponds, and she considered it more than likely that I would find a way to drown in one, if not both of them.

I'd meet the Lally Kids outside the church connected to our school. The three of them would trudge home wordlessly, with me bringing up the rear. I was annoyed at having to follow them home, and they were puzzled that I had to, but we all just followed orders.

I had two standing instructions from my mom upon learning I was going to be following them home every day after school: 1) never leave the Lallys and 2) never walk across the ice on the ponds. Ever.

These orders came into very clear conflict with practicality as soon as it got cold. Walking home one day, the Lallys began walking across one of the ice-covered ponds. I stopped at the edge.

The biggest turned around. He was much older, maybe a fifth grader.

"Well?"

"I can't walk across the ice."

"Are you scared?"

"No."

"Oh, come on. You're scared."

"No, really. My mom told me I couldn't."

He walked over to me, leaving his sisters on the ice. Lowering his voice so they couldn't hear, he said, "Here's some free advice. Never tell anyone that your mom said you can't do something."

"Why?"

"Because kids will beat you up."

"Really?"

"For sure. Definitely."

"Are you going to beat me up?" It seemed more than likely.

"No. I don't beat up first graders. And you're just a kid. And you're stupid."

Fearing it could be true, I said nothing. He went on.

"All kids are. When you're my age, you'll just know stuff."

"OK."

"So are you coming?"

"Can I just walk around?"

"No. Takes too long."

I looked out at the silvery ice stretched before me and then back at him.

"OK, I'll go."

"Good kid."

So for the first time I could remember, I deliberately disobeyed my mother. We walked across the ice that time and many times after that, and while nothing bad ever happened, I would look longingly at the big stone bridge across the pond and hope the ice melted soon, so I wouldn't be such a bad boy.

"Don't tell your mom," he said.
"OK."
"Only a fink tells his mom."
"OK."
"OK."

Kathy would invariably be doing wash or cleaning when I came in. She was always cleaning, and she usually seemed a bit surprised and pissed off to see me. Back then, we lived in a regular house type of house, but you would have thought it was a mansion based on how much cleaning she did. Not only was she always cleaning, she was always telling you about how much she had cleaned. She'd run down the list of what she had cleaned and where in the house you were now not allowed to go.

"Sean, is that you?" Yelling from somewhere upstairs.

"Yeah." I'd be at the back door, taking off my shoes and anything on me that might have acquired dirt during the day so as to prevent any sort of transfer onto something of my mother's.

"Don't go in the living room."

"OK."

The radio would be tuned to WNEW from New York. It was on every day, and the DJ was Scott Muni doing the afternoon drive. He had a voice like a thousand cigarettes talking to you. It was the classic rock station, but this was back when that didn't mean they played crappy old greatest hits records. They played everything.

My parents had a whole cabinet full of records, and when they went out and left me with a babysitter, I'd sit there and spread them out all over the living room floor. Record covers were big, but they were even bigger when you were six. They took up your whole range of vision when you held them a foot away from your face.

I wasn't that with-it as a kid, and questions weren't really encouraged around the house, so I'd sit and wonder what those freaky looking English guys were doing crossing the street, and where that freewheelin' young guy with the gorgeous happy girl on his arm in the snow was going. But I wanted to hang out with those two guys with the guitar and the saxophone, one leaning on the other, best pals. They looked like a pair that never had a bad time and rarely put those instruments down and couldn't give a shit about anything, the one fella looking at the other with a face saying, "How great is this?"

Most of the albums were my mom's and those were a lot of the Beatles and Simon & Garfunkel, and those were OK. She'd sing "Kodachrome" and "Penny Lane" while running the vacuum. But Mike only listened to two bands: the Rolling Stones and Springsteen.

The old man's devotion to both was such that other music went largely unrecognized. He never once put anything else on, ever. The glove compartment of his car was jammed with tapes, and every single goddamn one of them was one of those two bands. Mick and Bruce could have released a tape of a farting contest, and he'd have bought it. Other music would be on, and it was like he couldn't hear it, but turn on "Street Fighting Man," and he'd be shadow boxing all over the house.

Before going upstairs and facing my mom after school, I'd sit on the first step so I could hear Scott Muni talking and try to guess the next song he'd play. I never once got it right, but I would sit and whisper, "'I Can't Explain' . . . 'Eight Days a Week' . . . no, 'She's the One . . .'" and Muni would come on and say something like, "Here we go with a great sound, a great record, this is Neil Young with 'Heart of Gold.'" The way he introduced a song made you want to pump your fist a little bit, because he was so excited about it, and now you were excited about it, too.

"Damn, 'Heart of Gold,'" I'd whisper, and head up the stairs.

My idea of a good day after school consisted of watching "Star Blazers" at four-thirty on Channel 11 and then reading in my room.

This is the God's honest truth. I wanted a half hour of a Japanese cartoon about a ship sent from Earth to conquer an alien race bombarding us with radioactive rocks, and then I wanted to sit in my room with the door closed and read books. I was a total loser.

My mom realized my failure and tried to normalize me. I'd try to sneak by her while she was cleaning the bathroom, hoping that maybe she'd forgotten I was home, but the old lady never would.

"How was school?"

"Good."

"OK, what are you going to do now?"

This was a loaded question, because she knew exactly what my intentions were, and I knew exactly what she was going to say. We did this dance almost every day.

"I have some stuff to read." This was not a lie. My room was full of stacks of books in alphabetical order lining the walls. They were the only decorations I really had, aside from my box of records upon which sat my record player.

And so it came. "Why don't you go out and play with your friends?"

Gut punch.

"Can I just stay in today? I think it's going to rain."

"What? It's not going to rain. Go on, get out there. Make some friends. You have to learn to play with other kids."

I'd loiter as long as I could in my room before she threw open the door and told me to get going. It was useless to argue, there was no way I could stay. A side effect of this daily confrontation was that it made me pray for rainy days for the rest of my life, a condition I still enjoy suffering from. There's nothing like a guilt-free day inside with no reason to go anywhere or do anything.

The kids in my neighborhood never went to the park. They played on the golf course behind a row of houses where there was a big open field. We weren't really allowed there, and every so often, we'd see one of the club employees coming across the grass on a golf cart at us, looking angry and pathetic as he approached us from hundreds of feet away at about five miles an hour. Everyone would scatter as if he were the cops, running into the woods or neighboring backyards, but there was no danger the pimply-faced caddy would or could do anything past telling us to get lost.

I'd leave through the back door of our house and run past the never-used swing set that Mike had put in years before and still pointed to as proof positive that he participated in our development. There was a woodpile adjacent to the fence covered in leaves obscuring the secret life of worms. I'd hop over it, landing one foot on the top of a cedar fence, and leap into the neighbors' backyard before running down their driveway and across the street into a stand of trees. A few feet in and you'd find a path leading up to a chain-link fence, the kind covered in thin green rubber and easily penetrable to anyone and anything possessing hands or hooves, and therefore totally useless.

There, in the big field, would be a group of about ten kids from the surrounding neighborhood, usually covered in mud by the time I arrived. The thing was, none of them were my friends. Their moms knew my mom, and moms had a habit of saying things like, "We just moved here, and Little Johnny has no friends yet," and the other one says, "Well, he should play with Bob and Joe," and before you know it you're standing awkwardly on their front doorstep, ringing the bell and asking if they're home. My mom actually put me up to this when we moved to the neighborhood, and it probably made going to pick up a girl at her parents' house years later that much easier, because not much is worse than being six or seven years old and having to stand on some other kid's doorstep with snot on your nose to ask if he wants to play. The embarrassment is horrible, especially when it becomes very clear that the other kid's mom has never mentioned your existence.

And that was how I "knew" most of the kids at the golf course playing Kill the Man with the Ball. We all knew they didn't want me there and I didn't want to be there. But we went through the motions, and by "motions," I mean I instantly became the Man with the Ball.

Three things were against me. I was very small for my age, I had a big mouth, and I could take a lot of pain. The last two came in handy when I finally grew and was able to dispense punishment on the field, but for now, I was the one taking it. I'd swear the green grass yellow; I'd learned a lot from the old man on the odd weekend he was home. I learned that using the f-word and something female together worked wonders—motherfucker, fucking bitch, whorefuckingassholemother-fuckingbitch, etc.

My life has been far from cursed, and I generally consider myself to be one of the luckier people on the planet, but there's nothing quite like the resentment you feel when ten kids are knocking the shit out of you and all you wanted to do was stay home. Even then I had a feeling that there were parents out there who would think that was pretty great. I just wanted to be left alone, and now, more than not being left alone, I was going to get a brutal ass-whupping.

That was the way it went most of the time. I'd come home covered in dirt and grass stains in the summer and mud stains in the fall and spring. Mom would make me stand at the back door and put all my dirty clothes in the washer before I ran up to my room in my underwear, tighty-whiteys of course, as if more shame were needed.

She never thought it odd that I came home looking like I'd just tried to break a horse every day. She'd had five brothers, a few of whom went to the military, so she figured boys just naturally kicked the shit out of one another. So my bloody noses and bloody lips and torn ears and muddy faces never really fazed the old lady.

One night, though, the old man came home early. I was walking up the driveway, and I saw his car parked by the side of the house. Sometimes there was a cop car with him. He was a prosecutor then, and there had been threats. This time I just saw his car sitting next to the house, and I snuck around it to the back door and quietly opened it so I could slip out of my muddy clothes without him seeing.

I was unlucky.

"What the fuck happened to you?"

The old man knew what it looked like when a kid had had hell kicked out of him, because he'd kicked hell out of plenty of people.

"We were playing up at the golf course."

"Playing what?"

"Football."

"Football? Were YOU the fucking ball?"

"No."

"Well, what happened?"

At this point my mom came in to the kitchen and started explaining about how I played with my friends every afternoon and this was the way boys played.

"Kath, please." She kind of threw up her hands and walked into the living room.

He turned back to me. "Come on outside."

We went out into the backyard, and it had gotten cold. The sweat and the mud caught the chill and sent it straight down my back as we stood just beyond the little squares of yellow light thrown by the kitchen lights on the grass.

"So?" He looked down at me, and while I'm sure most people always remember their father being ten feet tall, in my memory he was taller than the house. He had a way of filling up everything you saw, sucking any bravery or self-confidence or falsehood right out of you and making you wish you could shit your pants, just so you'd have something else to talk about.

"They're bigger than me."

"Well. No shit."

"They are. And it's just all of them against me."

"Why's that?"

"They don't like me."

"Why don't they like you?"

"Because I don't want to be there."

"Why don't you want to be there?"

"They're not my friends. I told Mom, I just want to sit in my room."

"Right," he said, cocking his eyebrow and pacing thoughtfully. He pulled me over to the car, picked me up and put me on the hood of it. It was still warm from the driving. My feet rested on the bumper, and he leaned against it next to me.

"Listen. I don't care if you don't have any friends. I only ever had a few friends in my whole life, and I never really liked them. And I don't care if you want to sit in your room and read Joe's old books all day. Maybe you'll turn into something better than another fucking lawyer." His hand on my shoulder now, turning me to his face, a face that glowed red with any emotion, but particularly with anger.

"You can't just let these kids kick you around. Is that what happens?"

"Yeah. There's ten of them."

"Ever hit any of them back?"

"Yeah."

"Well?"

"Yeah, well, you hit one of them, and then the rest of them just jump on you."

"Listen, I've got work to do."

"OK." I could feel the shame well up in my guts, I felt sick of myself. He probably felt sick just looking at me. He ran his hands along the hood of the old yellow Toyota he'd bought from our neighbor, despite the wires that hung down off the dash and the sticky clutch, and then walked to the house. He opened the screen door and turned back to me. For a few seconds he was quiet, looking not at me but over me.

Then his eyes focused on me. "You want to know something? You don't have to fight them all. Just kick the shit out of one of them. Word gets around."

I thought about it in the driveway, leaning against the car. Maybe he thought I might amount to something after all.

It was another week or so before I had to go back to the golf course. It rained, and I was in my element, as it were. I stayed up in my room flipping through Mike's old encyclopedias from when he was a kid. I'd come across them while staying over at Joe's house, in Mike's old room. This was the same room I'd spent years of nights sleeping in before my grandfather absentmindedly said to me one day, "So what do you make of the secret room?"

"What?"

"Ohhhhh, yeah. Secret room. Maybe I never mentioned it.'

He had to be kidding. Secret rooms are probably one of the top ten best things ever if you're under the age of ten. It calls to mind castles and hangings and dungeons.

"It's in the closet." In the closet? In what closet? The closet with all the mothball-smelling remnants of every suit, shirt and pair of nasty old basketball sneakers Mike ever wore? That closet?

I ran up the three flights of stairs, threw open the door, shoved the stuff hanging down to the side, and there, at the back of the closet, was a tiny door, smaller even than me. I thought of hobbits. There could be anything in there. Maybe hobbits.

He stepped past me and put an ancient key into the door and flung it open. It was dark. It smelled like an old gym, like wood and mildew and dirty clothes. He crawled in, and I stooped in after him. The light still worked.

Laid out before me was all that remained of my old man's childhood. Model ships and airplanes lay beside toy trains and basketballs. There were toy guns, rifles, handguns, even a replica cannon.

Grandpa laughed. "Wow, look at this." He began picking items up at random and declaring when they'd been purchased.

"Christmas, 1954. Christmas, 1957. His birthday, 1955. Oh, damn. 1960, his own goddamn basketball. He used this cannon to shoot Sue in the ass. Goddamn kids."

He turned around, hands full of toys. "What are you doing?"

I was sitting in the corner, hands full of encyclopedia.

"I'll never figure you out, kid."

It rained for days, and I almost made it through D. What a colossal nerd.

On a Wednesday, the sun rose in its bloated and eye-pinching way. I was disgusted.

That day, after school, she was waiting. I knew nothing could save me, not even Scott Muni and the classic rock sounds of WNEW.

"It's such a nice day out," she said. She was just taunting me now.

"OK, I'll go play."

"Yeah, you've got to get out of the house." She couldn't let you just agree, she had to let you know you were doing it regardless of your thoughts on the matter.

I trudged up to the field. I'd thought a bit about what Mike had said, and somewhere inside of me, I just knew I wasn't up to it.

The game was in full swing when I arrived, as it always was. I didn't exactly rush. This was a game with no official start and no official stop. It ended when you had to go home, and I just tried to stick around long enough for no one to think I was a total pussy or until I thought I'd be allowed back into the house, whichever came first.

There was a delicate ballet going on within the total violence of Smear the Queer. The dance went like this: you tried to avoid being anywhere near the ball while trying to look like you weren't really trying to do that at all. The Dance of the Passive-Aggressive. At some point it all broke down, though, and the football would come flying out towards you, usually having exploded out of the hands of some kid who had just gotten pummeled.

As I walked toward the scrum, the ball hit me in the face and fell into my hands. I could absolutely believe my luck. I had a second to look up and see the horde coming towards me before I was engulfed. I could feel them on top of me and the cold wet squish of the mud in my face. The air choked out of me, and all I could think of was how unfair it all was and how much I wanted to be anywhere else. The tackle was bad enough, but then they smacked you until the ball came out.

Everybody got up, and the game moved on. We ran around some more, and through the film of a painful head and the mud, I blindly tried to join in on the group tackles and general violence. But it was enough after a while, and as usual, I tried to skulk off towards the woods unseen or barely noticed. The closer I got, the faster I'd move, until I was almost to the spot in between the two big oak trees where I'd dash through them, pull up the chain link fence and rush through backyards and on to home.

As I hit the trees, Paul hit me. I fell back on my ass, shocked at first as he stood over me.

"Game's not over, asshole." He smiled his big toothy wolfish grin; he was a truly loathsome character. My head was rolling around on my shoulders now, and I could sense that the game behind me had stopped. There would be no skulking away from this. He stood there holding the ball out to me.

I got up, awkwardly. I must have looked like a crab trying to do a handstand. Not for the first time, I was conscious of my own ridiculousness.

"I'm going home."

Paul sneered. "Oh yeah? Afraid? Come on." He gestured towards the field.

"No."

"You're such a little bitch."

"Fuck you."

"Yeah?" He wound up and threw the ball at me as hard as he could. I put my arms out to catch it, expecting failure. Except this time, in the universe's own lazy way, things kind of went my way. The ball bounced off of my outstretched palms and straight into Paul's nuts.

"Awwwww, awwwwww, FUCK," he yelled, rolling back and forth. I leapt on the bastard, swinging my fists wildly, trying to get his face. I'd cheated, I'd hit him in the balls and had not even meant to, but this kind of cosmic justice only comes around every decade or so. There were cheers from the other kids, the bloodthirsty rabble that they were, and I still think of that whenever someone goes on about the innocence of youth and all. I went for his eyes, punching all around them, until I could see his face looked like a plate after a summer barbecue.

It wasn't righteous anger, or pent up bitterness, or anything else even close to rage that made me jump on him. I just wanted to go home, and I hated these kids and their fucking game and their golf course and the smell of wet grass and the mud and the snot and the freezing cold when God had given us perfectly functional couches and perfectly awesome Japanese cartoons to watch inside.

I sat up and rolled off, into the mud. We were both covered in it, but Paul's face was streaked with blood. I could see it running down into his hair. He kept on swearing and rolling around and holding his face. Ignoring the crowd, I pulled myself out of the mud and walked back to the trees. I was a mess.

They looked at me, dumbly. "Fuck all this shit," I yelled.

At the back door, I stripped off my muddy clothes and threw them in the washer. Dinner was on. Mom saw me try to streak past her in the kitchen.

"Your father's coming home for dinner." This meant a few things, among them: clean yourself up, hurry up about it, and act happy when he gets here.

I ran up the stairs in my underwear to the bathroom and threw on the shower, but not before catching a look at my hands. Quickly, I pulled them away from the water. Staring down at my knuckles, I saw that they were still covered in blood. There was no goddamn way I was washing that off. Mike was going to see this.

I walked downstairs and sat at the table, waiting for him, admiring my bloodstained hands. I didn't even notice my mother standing behind me.

"Jesus, what happened?"

I put my fists in my lap. "Nothing."

She grabbed at them and pulled them into the light. "What the hell did you do to yourself?"

"Nothing, Mom." It was useless explaining the code of the jungle to this woman; she'd never understand the things warriors like Mike and I got up to outside of this house.

"Go back upstairs and wash that off."

"No, just leave it. I want to keep it."

"What? That's disgusting. Clean it off. Hurry up."

"Mom, come on."

"Get up there, hurry up, NOW."

"Fiiiiiiiiiiiiiiiine." I trudged up the stairs. In the bathroom I watched as the water washed the streaks of blood and mud down the drain. There were still cuts on my fingers and knuckles from Paul's face, but nothing as dramatic as what had come off. I sat down on the edge of the tub and wondered if there was any way I could beat up Paul again so I could show the old man I'd finally stood up to them.

That night at dinner I thought to tell him. It never came up. In the kitchen, putting everything in the dishwasher, I could hear him talking to another lawyer on the phone, and heard him end the conversation as he so often did, "Remember, we're the good guys."

I looked at him standing there on the phone and thought maybe I'd tell him when he hung up.

But I didn't.

Chapter 8

WHEN I DIED

Kathy says I love the water. She says all I wanted to do was come down here to look at it.

Oh yeah, man. You love the water. You don't own a boat and you're a shit swimmer, but you love the water.

Did I teach you to swim?

I sure hope not. You did teach me the value of knowing how to swim, though.

If you've never been on the Point Pleasant boardwalk in the morning during the fall, I highly recommend you make amends and get there. There were a few times in my life when I felt like the curtains had parted on my old man's life and I had seen a bit of the real him, and one of those times was right here on the boardwalk, a few days after Mike's accident. I was driving from the house to the hospital when I saw the tops of all of those goofy amusement park rides and decided to take that right turn that took me to them.

It had been years since I'd been to the boardwalk and no matter what has come and gone since, I still get excited about it. You can smell the place as soon as you get out of the car, a smell like popcorn and bubblegum. Stepping down those weathered two-by-fours brings back memory after memory. There I am on the bumper cars yelling at everyone because some kids ganged up on me and kept smashing into my car. There's the little midget Ferris wheel that looked a hundred feet high when I was a kid, the one I refused to ever get on. There were the little cars that just went around and around. I preferred these because they were harmless and not that fast or scary. I would go on them mostly to appease my parents, who had taken us to the boardwalk to have fun, damn it, so we'd better have some.

The truth is that I never liked the rides; I just liked to look at them. They were always too fast or too slow or filled with too many kids. I liked to sit on the bench and watch everyone go by, eating and laughing and generally looking too happy, but looking the kind of happy that you could never take your eyes off of.

The greasy pizza joints were all boarded up because it was still early, but I looked inside, and in the midst of the small forest of stacked chairs, there was the giant disturbing clown sitting on a box that would be filled with popcorn in the summer and surrounded by screeching, blubbering children while the Italian guys yelled at you to come and get your pizza.

There are rows of benches that line the fence on the boardwalk. They face out to the water onto a beach that seems impossibly huge. Most beaches I've seen in New Jersey are about fifty feet from the dune to the water. In Point Pleasant, you could build a football stadium on the giant patch of sand separating the boardwalk from the water. I sat down on one of the benches and looked out at the glare coming off of the sun hitting the water. It had only been up for a few hours, so its brightness still dominated the sky.

To my left was a jetty with a miniature lighthouse atop it. It was a fake lighthouse, it didn't even look like a real one. It was really just metal bars all welded together with a green light and a red light at the top of it. Could it have cost them that much more to make a cool-looking authentic lighthouse out there? No. But this was New Jersey, so they'd half-assed it and put up something merely pragmatic instead. The jetty consisted of a big ramp made of concrete surrounded by T-shaped concrete blocks that buffered it from the current. The waves would slap against them and throw up huge splashes of foam into the air and all over the jetty.

It didn't always look like that. Mike used to take us there once every summer for a day he called "The Trip to the Big Rocks." Mike acted like this was a trip to Disneyworld. He'd put it on his calendar, and the night before he'd pack up all his camera gear. He got oddly excited for it, probably because the few actual family vacations we did take usually ended in some sort of Griswoldian disaster. A trip six miles up Route 35 seemed very doable by comparison, and it was something everyone could agree to.

When we were kids, the T-shaped things weren't there—instead it was surrounded by real rocks, each one the size of a Chevy. They formed little caves all around the jetty, the floors of which were wet sand. Long strands of seaweed hung down, and there were little pools of water with live starfish clinging to the rocks. I never even saw dead starfish anywhere else at the beach, so the idea of living ones right there in front of you gave it the feel of an aquarium you could play in without anyone else around.

We'd go out there early in the morning, around seven before the beach people had arrived and it was relatively deserted. We'd run around through the rock caves, and my sisters would screech whenever a big wave would spray us. Mike would make us come up on the jetty whenever he'd had enough of waiting, and we were made to stand there while he took pictures of us smiling. He'd take so many that your face hurt from holding your fake smile, and then he'd yell "Smile!" until you managed to get a more lifelike smile on your face as you squinted into the sun.

I did everything I could to get it over with, forcing my eyes open and plastering a big stupid smile on my face so he could snap away and we could head to a pancake restaurant just off of the boardwalk. We'd have to wait in line, and by the time you got in there after standing in the heat, maybe pancakes weren't tops on your list. But they were so good, you didn't care. My littlest sister would sit there chewing away, and the chewing itself would be the worst part about the trip. The kid chewed like a gerbil—squishing the food to the side of her mouth and moving her teeth together up and down insanely fast. I would whisper to her that I was going to pour syrup over her head and stick a pancake to her face, and she'd look over with her little full cheeks and say, "Ohhhhhhh. No?"

One day there was a nor'easter coming off the coast. These were vicious storms, but among Nolans it was considered incredibly pussified to ever flee anything having to do with weather. So we all stayed down at the beach house while everyone else with a sense of self-preservation fled inland. I was sitting on the couch reading when Mike came down from his office and said, "Let's go to the Big Rocks."

Mom heard him from the other room, and said, "Michael, you're insane." He was, but he knew I'd say yes anyway. He had emerged from his office in a ridiculous outfit—full head to toe bright yellow rain gear. He was carrying his camera. "This is going to be great," he said. "Sean, put on your rain gear."

"I don't have any rain gear."

He took off his hooded rain jacket and put it on me. It was the size of a muumuu and came down past my knees. It was ridiculous-looking and even he laughed. "Wow," he said. He still had on his rain pants, and he threw on a totally inadequate windbreaker.

Over Mom's objections, we got in the car and drove down to the Big Rocks. The wind and rain had already started, but it wasn't close to how bad it would get. The rain began picking up as we reached the parking lot at the jetty and made our way out onto it, leaning into the wind. The ocean was no longer the deep blue it usually was. Now it was a roiling angry gray with dull green splotches and foam spread across its surface. The waves beat against the shore and the rocks, and the air was so wet that your face felt like you'd just gotten out of the shower. We got about three quarters of the way out onto the jetty when Mike yelled, "Turn around! I'll take your picture!"

The crashing waves sounded like artillery to my left, but this was Mike making the suggestion, so I guessed that he must know what he was doing. It also continued an established family practice of taking embarrassing pictures of the kids and pasting them on all the walls at home. There were pictures of me with Santa looking bored, pictures of me looking at a giant Easter Bunny like I was terrified—why not a picture in a muumuu during a nor'easter?

I stood lamely on the jetty while Mike focused the camera, trying to get the massive swells behind me into the shot. Before he could take it, he suddenly dropped the camera around his neck and charged at me, scooping me up and running for the fake lighthouse. Looking up past it into the water, I saw a massive wave about to crash on us. Mike threw us up against the cold wet metal bars of the lighthouse as it came down on us. I could feel the skin of my face being slapped and pulled by the water. It was everywhere around us, and I felt him push us even closer into the metal bars. I was crushed between him, the lighthouse and the water. I had that terrified feeling you get when water is rushing around you and you think it will never end, like when a wave catches you in the open and pushes you down into the sand. It churns and churns and feels like it will hold you down until you're forced to breathe water. And then it stopped.

When the giant wave subsided, we were shocked and soaked and sucking wind, literally. I looked around and saw two guys who had been fishing at the end of the jetty holding on to the bars of the lighthouse as tightly as we were. "Holy shit, oh, holy shit," one of them mumbled. Their bait, tackle and fishing poles had all been swept out into the ocean. Spray still flew from the waves crashing low against the rocks. Mike put me down for a second, turned me around and threw me over his shoulder in a fireman's carry. He turned to the two fishermen, who from my almost upside-down position I could see standing on the edge of the jetty looking out at the rocks for their lost gear.

"Guys, let's go!" It was his lawyer voice, and when you heard it, it carried a certain inevitability. They got moving. With the world upside down, we jogged down the jetty toward the parking lot. The waves shot up on either side, bringing a steady shower down upon us. Mike put me down when we reached the lot, and we looked back to see yet another wave coming that looked like it could take down the lighthouse. Had we still been there, we would have taken an out-and-out pasting from the water. We stared at the scene in dumb amazement for a moment. Then the fishermen went back to complaining about what they'd lost.

Mike and I got in the car, both of us shivering and breathing hard. I turned and saw that he was smiling. "Well," he said, "that certainly did not go as planned."

"I guess not." I smiled, too.

"Was that kind of stupid?"

I shook my head. "No, it was great. It could have killed us."

"Yeah, it really could have. How about that?"
"It was great."
"Don't tell your mother."
"No way."
He'd almost killed me. Now we had a secret.

Chapter 9

THESE DAYS NOTHING BUT SUNSHINE

So I wasn't exactly our first reason to go to the hospital, was I?

No, we make a lot of trips there.

You must hate it.

Some of them weren't all that bad.

Joe Nolan was a notorious ice cream fiend. I recall seeing news reports on crack addicts during the 1980s and thinking that the closest approximation to that in my experience would be Joe's jones for the cold stuff. You have to understand the power of ice cream in this man's life. If he had a choice, he'd have been in an ice cream store all day.

In Point Pleasant, there's an ice cream store on the highway called Hoffman's. It's one of the last places Joe and I went for ice cream that's still in business. Stores at the beach have a way of burning down or getting knocked over to become condos. There's more money in fire and flats than there is in cones.

There was Runaway Bay, which was really a bar, but had ten different flavors, none of which were particularly good. But as the man said, in the days of the frost you seek a minor sun. Across the street from Runaway was The Corner Store, where I first learned of the supremacy of mint chocolate chip ice cream. There really is no finer, and those that tell you different are likely not the kind of people you want to ask about anything else. The Store, as it was known to those in the know, those in the know being people who lived within a three block radius, was also just OK. The waitresses were always cute and tan and blonde, but they were local, they were older, and they knew you, so they all saw through you. You were just another cone to them.

The Store was only a few blocks from the beach and from our house, and Dad would occasionally stroll the whole family down after dinner in the summer. I had figured out early how to game the system. Cones were for fools; the true connoisseur went for the cup because you got more. The blonde would really pack it in, and you could get chocolate sauce on top without making a huge mess. Try packing ice cream into a cone; the thing will explode all over you.

Those two places were good for a utility ice cream run. But for the good stuff, Joe and I would beat it out of town and get out on the highway. Hoffman's was for driving. Joe and I would fly up Route 35 in the Cadillac, and if it was a good summer day, chances were better than fifty-fifty that we would end up at Hoffman's. Hoffman's was that little bit extra, our 11. If you had a day that just wasn't happening, if you'd been all over but never really ended up anywhere very good, if the weather was right, and cash was still king, well, that Caddy just might pull up outside of Hoffman's.

We'd drive to Hoffman's with Hal Roach narrating on the radio. Roach was an Irish comedian in the vein of Bob Hope. He spoke in a heavy accent with a fair amount of mumbling, and every joke began with, "So Murphy walks into a bar . . ." Murphy would invariably be a drunken idiot or encounter drunken idiots in said bar and lunacy would ensue. After each punchline, Roach would roar something like, "Thar she is, ladies and gentlemen! Write it down! Write it down! That one won't be back!"

Joe would guffaw and slap the steering wheel. He and Hal made for quite a Martin and Lewis combination as Joe would smack me on the shoulder and say, "Listen, go on, listen to this one." Hal would tell the joke, Joe would smash the steering wheel and turn and say, "That's good, that is a good one. Remind me to tell that one." The truth is I never could remember any of them then and I sure can't now.

Hoffman's was nondescript—a big wooden building and a parking lot with some benches. But for those who knew, Hoffman's was it. I'd have sworn they had two hundred flavors, and maybe they did. But only one mattered. Neither of us ever considered ordering anything else.

The front was always crowded with kids and their parents eating ice cream. Half the kids would be wearing most of it all over themselves. The stuff would be running down their arms, all over their shirts; they may as well have pied the kids in the face.

Joe hated sloppy children. "I mean, have you seen the way some people allow their children to eat? It's like a pig farm. Look at these children, covered in stuff. They've got their faces stuck into it. And then do you know what it tastes like, after you've done that?"

"No."

"Face! It tastes like face! Disgusting."

When we'd get home, his wife, Jeanne, would always interrogate us. "Were you two out for ice cream, driving around and wasting good money on getting fat?" She'd look us up and down. "Well, were you? Out for ice cream again? Out for a drive? Oh, Joe."

"No, Jeannie. Just out for some fun." The air conditioning was always on full blast in their house, so walking into the place on a summer's day was like walking into an icebox. It felt fantastic at first, but within an hour you had a long-sleeved shirt on you. In the back of my mind I thought maybe she did it on purpose. She was trying to make it cold so maybe Joe wouldn't crave ice cream so much. Sometimes, it seemed like she barely knew him.

Joe had his first heart attack when I was young. The call came, and we drove straight to the hospital. I remember feeling a sense of privilege, even ownership, as I was asked to get in the car late to go see him and my sisters were left at home.

This was hardly the time to ask Mike questions, and given that there never was a good time to ask him anything, I kept quiet. But he was talking to my mother. I heard the bit of doubt and concern in his voice, so uncommon that I struggled to identify what it was. I felt guilty for not having been there earlier as I pictured Joe sitting all alone in a hospital in the middle of the night.

There was a scene when we got there. Lawyers Joe knew stood around with their wives, looking ashen and worried. Some of them were smoking outside, while others just stood around staring at every doctor who came out of Joe's room. His personal doctor, Doctor Ryan was there, too.

None of the relatives had arrived, except, of course, my grand-mother, holding court and going on about the awfulness of it all. She rushed up to my father when we walked in. He told her to relax, and when he did, everyone else seemed to relax, too. It didn't have a thing to do with him being a lawyer or even the oldest son. I had a notion that this was his life, really. It was what set him apart from all the lawyers and the doctors. He had arrived, and when Mike Nolan ar-rived, the look on his face, the way he walked, the way he touched your shoulder and told you not to worry—every word, every action, said the same thing: "I'm here now. It's going to be fine. Leave it to me."

And they did. The small crowd parted as we walked in to see the doctors. Thinking on it later, no one had told us to enter. We just marched in and flagged one down.

The doctors looked grave . . . "very serious event" . . . "utmost dan-ger" . . . "we won't know for some time." They gave us the whole busi-ness. Little did I know how much of this I would hear in my life. It was all very interesting to me, but hardly a cause for worry. The old man was a tank. This would all boil down to minor annoyance for him. Mike didn't look worried either. He started making phone calls on the lobby pay phone. I sat with my mother while she read a magazine. I watched everything. Doctor Ryan sat down and asked me how I was feeling. I told him I was great because I didn't want him giving me a pill like Mom was always saying old people doctors do.

Doc went up to Mike while he was on the phone. Mike pulled the receiver down past his chin and gave him a look of total annoy-ance. "Yeah?" he asked, as if Doc was some kind of salesman at the front door.

"Well, Michael, do the doctors need anything from me? You know, as his primary physician, I . . ."

Mike looked at him as if he was considering whether to hit him in the face with the phone. "Please," was all he said before going back to his call. Doc left him alone.

We stayed all night, but I wasn't tired. I can stay up for hours in hospitals. I think it's the fluorescence, or maybe the smell. It was light when they finally came to talk to Mike. He walked outside with Mom. I sat and looked at the lights in the ceiling, noticing how the little bumps looked like the helmets of Army men marching off to war. I was always thinking things like that and forgetting I had thought them and then rediscovering that I had thought them months and years later.

Mom came back in and told me to go out with my dad. He was standing in the early morning sun in the parking lot. As usual, he wasn't saying anything, and I was left to stand there, waiting for the big man's pronouncement. And finally it came.

"So?" he said.

"What?"

"So? What do you think?"

"I don't know." I covered my eyes against the rising sun.

"He's going to be OK."

"So that's good, right?"

"It's really good. He's lucky. He's going to want you around later. But I just had a talk with your grandmother, and she's worried."

"Worried about what?"

"She thinks you're a bad influence on him."

"I am? How?"

"Well, you know. The ice cream and the always going out to eat. You know, she knows you two get up to no good. And when he gets out of here, she's going to need you to keep track of things like that. You two can't be going to the boardwalk and eating cotton candy and hot dogs all day like you did before. And you can't drive that car." He was smiling slightly.

Even he knew that this was a ridiculous situation.

"OK. But I don't drive the car."

He smiled and shook his head.

It was the first and only time he ever acknowledged that he knew I was driving that Cadillac all over New Jersey. A long time after it was all over, it occurred to me that the way Joe and I got along so well must have been painful to my father. He and I never did things like that.

I walked back in and sat down. There were people crying about family they'd come to see, and I wondered how many people had died within a hundred feet of me. I never liked people crying in public around me; even then I felt like it was somewhat embarrassing. It was like seeing pornography for the first time. It seems like something you shouldn't really be seeing, like something that should be happening in private. Only I got over the thing about pornography, but never the bit about the crying. I wondered—did these people not have any cars to cry in?

One of the guys who worked for Mike sat down next to me. I recognized him from the office as he waved over to Mike, who was back on the phone. "So, Sean—what did Mike say? What did he say about Joe? You know, I've been handling a lot of the case load at the office, and I . . ."

I looked at him like I might stab him with one of the nerdy pens he had stuck in his shirt pocket. "Please," I said to him before leaning back in my chair to look up at the little army men in the lights.

We went home for a bit. When we came back in the afternoon, they told us Joe was awake again, and I think they were all a little shocked that we didn't appear more relieved, especially when they'd done their best to scare the shit out of us in the morning.

They escorted us in this big room and there he was. It wasn't like the movies with tons of machines around him; there was just Joe and one machine that was relatively unimpressive. At that age, I judged coolness by how it compared to the cockpit of the Millennium Falcon—if it didn't have the same number of flashing lights and beeping things, it probably sucked.

The adults said their adult things, and then they left, and it was just the two of us. I sat on a plastic chair at the foot of his bed. He asked me how he looked. "Awful," I said.

His voice was raspy and struggling. "Do you think so?"

"Yeah."

"Soon it will be you. Look around, kid. This family spends a lot of time in the hospital. Don't think you're getting off easy."

"I'm healthy like a horse."

He slowly slapped the pillow lying across his chest. "Ha, good luck with that. How is your father doing? Worried?"

"He's talking to the doctors. They look worried."

"And he doesn't?"

I smiled.

"'Course he doesn't," Joe said. He looked around the room and out the window.

"I brought you something from the house." I held out his blue hat that read CAPTAIN. He wore it whenever he was out running errands, as if the checkout girls were suddenly going to start saluting him.

"Well, that is something, OK. Here now," and he put it on. "Excellent. Now I'll get some respect around here. How'd you get this?"

"I rode my bike over to the house, and one of the guys let me in. Then I rode back in time to leave with Mike and Kathy. I hid it in my jacket so Jeanne wouldn't see."

He was beaming. The man loved nothing better than a good bit of trickery.

"Good man," he said. This was his ultimate compliment. It was always said slowly, and usually before a plot was hatched. "I wonder now . . ."

"Yeah?"

"Well, I'm gonna be here for a while. The food in the place is disgraceful. You should see the lump of shit they tried to sell me as meatloaf. If you're going to feed me shit, just tell me, 'Mr. Nolan, this is shit. We know you paid good money to be here, but we're giving you shit. And that's just the way it is. And everyone else is enjoying their shit dinners as well, so you've nothing to complain about.' I would be fine with that. But don't tell me its meatloaf when I know damn well it's shit."

"Worse than Grandma's turkey?"

"Now you're just being a nasty little man."

"Yes."

"It's almost enough to make you wish the heart attack had done the job."

"Wow."

"They need Him in the kitchen."

"So?"

His eyes turned thin and sly. "If I'm in here for a while, I worry about Hoffman's going out of business." He raised a ". . . and you know what I'm talking about" eyebrow.

I smiled and nodded. "I could get over there."

He feigned shock. "Impossible. We've no way of getting you over there."

"Doc Ryan lives down the street. He'll be coming here every day. I could ask him to give me a ride and then stop at Hoffman's on the way over here. You know Mike will be going to the office from now on, and we won't need to look out for him anymore."

He thought about it. "What if you're caught? Jeanne will be looking out for you to do something sneaky."

"She won't look in my bag. If she finds it, I'll just say I was keeping it for later."

He did one of his snorts. "She won't buy that."

"Sure she will. She talked to Mike and he talked to me. She thinks that once she talks to him that she has nothing to worry about."

He laughed at my reading of the situation. "You've got a great future in the law. Here." He handed me twenty bucks from the roll of cash under his pillow. While I could never go through that kind of dough at the ice cream store, it was established custom in my family that when an adult gave a kid a too-large bill to go buy something, you were allowed to keep the change, no questions asked. There was no allowance, so this practice functioned as an informal allowance system. It also ensured that kids would be leaping at the chance to go down to the store for things. It was not uncommon to see one of my sisters make a face when she was asked to go get milk and given only a fiver. A ten-spot seemed much more sporting, but Mom could sometimes be a bit stingy with the dough, having grown up with not a whole lot of it. I took the twenty, wondering how much ice cream the man could possibly consume on a daily basis.

So that afternoon I was at Doc Ryan's, knocking on the door, asking about when he would be going to the hospital. He answered the door, and I could tell he was mildly surprised to see me but trying not to show it. His pale jowly face was hanging, and his eyes were at half-mast. I asked if he was going to the hospital tomorrow.

"Tomorrah an' every day after," came the response. He leaned down a bit to something approaching my height. "I'm the family doctor, you see. Joe needs me, and naturally I'll be there to offer whatever insight I can to the attending physician and so on and so on," he said with a regal wave of his hand. "My expertise may be required in light of Joe's . . . unfortunate condition."

"Well, do you think I can get a lift over with you?"

"Your parents aren't going?"

"Nah." Huge lie.

"Well, I imagine it would be important for Joe. There is a mental aspect to this, of course." He looked absent-mindedly out at the street.

The next morning I was waiting. It was ten in the morning, and I sat in his driveway, not too far from ours. When I told Mom I was getting a ride over with Doc Ryan, there had been all kinds of questions, most having to do with, "What are you up to and why?" but I had lied my way out of it. I sat in Doc's drive in my awful little shorts with a white T-shirt on. Mom was into the white T-shirt look for me, and this being the early 80s, it was a fairly popular thing at the Shore. I waited for fifteen minutes and then banged on the door. Nothing. The car was in the driveway, so I knew the old man was around. The door was open so I went in. When you come in to a house down at the beach, especially one of the old dark ones like Doc lived in, it takes a second for your eyes to adjust from the glare of the sun outside, and at first you can't see at all. When my eyes finally worked again, there was Doc, sitting on a huge captain's chair with Frank Sinatra blasting through the house.

I must have made some noise because he leapt to his feet and said, "Oh, hey! Sean. Very good. Time to go," and with that he got up from the chair and walked into the bathroom where I heard the shower go on.

Doc didn't drive a Cadillac. He drove something more like a Buick. The distinction means little to most people, but for us it was an issue of pride. The Cadillac radiated a certain sense of historic cool, while the Buick just said you were old. When you see a neighbor buy a Buick, you know he's just given up. It's like watching a thirty-something guy buy a minivan. You can almost see the forlorn look of "Show's over" on his face when he sees it in the driveway.

We turned up Route 35 toward the hospital. I had thought about how to persuade him that it was in his best interest to stop at Hoffman's on the way. I could tell him the truth. He'd fight it initially, based upon some half-remembered medical knowledge, but then if I told him that Joe said to do it, he'd fall in. He'd protest and yell and tell Joe he was killing himself, but in the end, he'd do what Joe wanted, because in the end, everyone did what Joe wanted. I decided to spare Joe the drama of Doc's scolding and just do the right and sensible thing, which was to lie.

"Can we stop at Hoffman's on the way? Mom said I could, and she gave me money for an ice cream."

"Heh?" he said, and the car swerved slightly.

"Hoffman's. In Point Pleasant. The ice cream store."

"Ice cream? Jesus, this country is headed to hell. You kids with ice cream at ten o'clock in the goddamn morning. Who eats ice cream at this hour?" Doc shouted out every word like we were in a crowded bar with the jukebox all the way up.

"So? We can stop?"

The old man had a moment of clarity just then. "You're not buying stuff for Joe, are you? It'll kill him. He's not meant to be eating ice cream after a heart attack." He looked over at me. "I know he's got you and everyone else fooled, but the man is not going to live forever. So no ice cream for him."

"No," I said. "Of course not." I put on my most serious face, but inside I was laughing like a hyena. Of course I was getting it for Joe. Did he think I'd have the balls to go to Hoffman's, get some for myself, and then show up in Joe's room empty-handed and smelling like mint chocolate chip ice cream? Did I have a fucking death wish?

Doc would never get it, and I would never explain it. But I did keep on gazing at him from the passenger seat with the look that had been passed from Joe to Dad and now to me. It was a stare, but a particularly dead-eyed one. You lowered your eyes to half-mast and then just looked at your victim. Joe had taught me once that if you really wanted to stare a person down, you looked at the forehead, not directly into the eyes. It made it all easier. From where I was sitting, I couldn't see most of Doc's forehead, so I just looked at his ear.

He finally looked over at me. "OK, all right. Jesus. Fine. We'll get ice cream."

We pulled into Hoffman's, and I grabbed my bag. "I'll be right out, Doc. Do you want anything?"

"Well, OK. How about Rocky Road with chocolate sprinkles?"

I didn't say anything. I could have slapped him. Sprinkles? I mean, SPRINKLES? Who could even ask for them with a straight face? And what kind of a made-up flavor was Rocky Road? I do believe it contained marshmallows. Disgraceful. There was no way I was going to ruin the good names of both myself and Joe Nolan by walking into a Hoffman's store staffed by kids unable to secure better paying jobs on the Boardwalk and bring ruin and mockery upon the family name by ordering sprinkles and marshmallows.

I came out with the two cones. Safely stuffed in my bag were a large container with five scoops of the green stuff and a cone wrapped in about twenty napkins to prevent it being crushed. Getting the cone separately had taken a bit of negotiation with the kid at the counter, but I'd explained the situation.

I handed Doc his cone.

"What's this?" he said.

"What?"

"This isn't Rocky Road and there's no sprinkles."

I tried to give him the stare again. "They were out of Rocky Road. And sprinkles."

"Really? At Hoffman's?"

"Yeah. So I just got you what I get."

"Oh. Well, thanks. Shitsville, I tell you. Nothing works in this country anymore. Not even ice cream."

When we got to the hospital, my main concern was getting Doc out of the way so I could deliver the goods without finding a big blob of melt in my bag. We hung about the waiting room before they told us we could go in, and there were still some of the guys from Joe's office milling around. I sat there, nervously eyeing my bag and wondering what sort of condition the green stuff was in. It wasn't long before Joe's nurse came in and told us he was up.

Jeanne was in the room. She gave a big hello, but I kept my distance to avoid her smelling the mint on me. I'd just destroyed an entire cone, and there was no way I'd come away from a solid pound of frozen sugar and chocolate smelling like roses. She'd know instantly. The woman could smell cigarettes, alcohol and mint chocolate chip ice cream from ten feet away. I lurked near the door, awash in minty shame.

The adults made small talk while I kept trying to catch Joe's eye to remind him I had the prize. I would put myself up on my tiptoes to try to catch his eye, but I was either too short or he really was wrapped up in a conversation with Doc about his health, which would be a shame. He wasn't taking the hint.

Finally he asked Doc to drive Jeanne home. Jeanne came out with, "Oh, Joe! I can get another ride home. I'll stay the afternoon." No, Joe insisted, she was probably tired from the late nights and early mornings. Jeanne began more than half her sentences with, "Oh, Joe!" It was like she was shocked each time she spoke to him.

They left, and I hopped up on the chair by the bedside, probably looking like something out of Alice in Wonderland, small in a giant doctor's chair. Joe donned the Captain's hat. "Court is in session," he said.

"I got the stuff."

"Great. Just great. Hold on." He got out of bed and went to the door. Opening it slowly, he looked either way down the hallway for Jeanne. "We're in the clear!" he said. He pulled one of the chairs from against the wall and shoved it under the door, like in the movies. "So where is it?"

"I hid it in my bag."

"Smuggling, great."

I took it out and put it on the little table next to his bed.

"Oh, jeez." he said. "Excellent work." It was then that I laid the coup de grace upon the table—the cone. He picked it up like it was a foreign object. "Good man. Impressive. Remind me to have more heart attacks." He took a spoon he'd saved from lunch and used it to put the ice cream in the cone. It didn't look half bad. Some of it was melted, but the overall survival rate was pretty good. I'd have eaten it. Between huge bites of the cone, he said, "I haven't had any of this stuff in days. You already had one?"

"Yeah."

He considered what had not made it onto his cone. "You want the rest of what's in here?"

"Oh yeah."

There was total silence as we went to work until a knock came at the door.

"The sawbones!" Joe roared in a whisper. He looked like a squinty pirate. "Go out and talk to him while I finish this."

I threw the ice cream on the table and ran for the door. The lucky thing was that there was a little hallway just before it that made the room slightly L-shaped. From the door, you couldn't see the person in bed. I opened the door, and there was some doctor, smiling. He made to walk past me, but I stepped in his way. Out of the corner of my eye, I could see the old man taking huge bites of the cone. I thought I could hear chocolate chips bouncing off the walls while he went to town on that cone, but if the doctor saw him eating it, I'd be banned from the hospital and Jeanne would set up an impenetrable security ring around him. He'd sink into a sullen, ice cream-less depression. It would be weeks or months before he was able to get out again, and I'd be stuck at home. I might have to get a job.

The doctor looked down at me blocking his way with an expectant face. I scrunched up my face a bit, to simulate emotion. I thought of Jeanne saying, "Oh Joe!" when she found out about what would thenceforth be known only as The Heart Attack on a Cone Incident, and I think my face registered the appropriate level of sadness.

The doctor said, "Are you alright, son?"

"Well, doctor," I said, motioning him back out into the hallway, "Do you think Grandpa will be OK? Is he going to live?" I swear I heard Joe giggling behind me, eating away.

"I think if your grandpa takes care of himself, he could live for a good long time." He went on with this, about hearts and exercise and attention to health, but I heard none of it. All I could think of was how annoying it was to be around adults who talked to you like a child, and was Joe going to eat the bit of ice cream I had left on the table.

From inside the room Joe came to the rescue. "Oh, doctor? Are you there?" We walked back inside. The doctor and Joe were all smiles. I just sat in the chair looking up at the lights again, knowing that I was years away from my first heart attack. Eventually, the doctor turned to me.

He smiled, "Don't worry, son. Grandpa will be back and strong like bull."

"Strong like matador," Joe corrected. "The bull always loses."

The doctor looked like a kid after some bully knocked his cone to the ground. "Well. OK. Very good," he stammered, and left.

Chapter 10

PASSENGER SIDE

What made hanging out with Joe so much fun?

He was always up to something. He constantly had something going on, no matter when you caught him. There was always a plan afoot to try to one up somebody, or sneak out for ice cream, or sit around watching a football game. The guy was never boring.

Was I boring?

No, man. You were focused.

Which means boring?

You were . . . focused.

Joe Nolan loved a good conspiracy. Always on the up-and-up himself, he longed to be master of the Big Game, to be one of the Guys in the Know, to be a fixer. Often when we were somewhere together and a group of guys would talk about some government fat cat doing dirty deals or some mob guy who was screwing people, he would nod along quietly, and as if he knew something they didn't. So when he called the house one day and said in a hushed voice, "Be outside in half an hour. I've just had an idea," I knew he thought he'd had a stroke of genius.

He did the usual slow pull into the driveway, only this time, he was moving with a purpose. I watched him from the front window on the street side as he leapt out of the car and ran towards the front door. I called to Kathy that I was leaving with Joe and ran downstairs.

He was standing there about to knock on the big captain's head doorknocker. "Let's go," he said. "This could be one of the best things I've ever thought of. I can't believe it took me this long to think of it."

He fancied himself something of a hidden genius when it came to the acquisition of "stuff." From boats to cars to new toilets, he really believed he had an angle on the other guy when it came to getting them.

We each walked to our respective spots in the car, me taking a bit longer to open and close the giant me-sized doors on the Cadillac while simultaneously hopping up on the seat. It all had to be done in one fluid motion with Tarzan-swinging-on-a-vine-like dexterity, or I risked closing the door on myself and falling out of the car completely.

We got out on the highway. "I just noticed something today. You know something? I've never won a thing in my life. Never. Did you ever notice that?"

"No, I guess not. But what do you mean? You've got tons of stuff."

"I bought all of that. I never won anything." He was smiling as he said it, leaning back in the seat and driving with his one hand on the big wheel of his big car as we ran down Route 35. I looked at him across the couch-like expanse—in my memory he seems to be a good fifteen feet away from me because the seat was that big.

"What do you have to win? You can buy almost anything, right?"

He laughed and pounded on the steering wheel. "Not anything, but a good amount of something, all right." We pulled past the church he and Jeanne went to and took a left onto the side street. He parked about ten car lengths down from the church. We were parked like a couple of cops on a stakeout. He hunched down so no one could see us.

The church was an old brown clapboard number built of wood with round windows. I had always hated it. It looked like a Protestant church that Catholics had taken over. There was no stained glass; there was no marble or stone. It was wooden and spare and hardly seemed to me even as a kid to be the kind of place God would want to hang out in—at least not a decent Catholic God, anyway.

"See that?" he said, nodding towards the church. He pointed at a gleaming white Cadillac parked in the grass in front of the church.

Every year Joe's church would raffle off a brand new Cadillac as a fund-raiser. They'd park it out front in June, right on Route 35, and the raffle would be in August. Most of the people attending Joe's church were some serious geriatric cases, so the priests knew their clientele enough to know that a Caddy was the thing to be parking out front. Every Sunday you'd see the old folks in their stretch pants and plaid shirts and awful hats out there buying tickets. It was an affluent crowd, but there was no doubt that a bunch of them really wanted that car. They got into it in the absent-minded way old people do—it's not like a lot of them had much else to think about.

"You see it? The car?" He was giddy now.

"Sure." I was straining to look above the dashboard, watching the line of white-haired men and women in their Sunday polo shirts and neckties filing past the card table where two old ladies were selling the raffle tickets.

"Every year now with that raffle, and I've never won a damn thing. Never once won a damn thing for myself. That's going to change."

I thought about it for a minute while watching the old people coming and going. They bought tickets, and walked over to check out the car they might win.

"Grandpa, you already have a Cadillac." We were sitting in it.

"Yes, I do." He was barely paying attention to me. He was too busy staring at the Caddy.

"And you could buy another, right?'

"Sure, I guess."

"Have you ever even bought tickets for the raffle before?"

"Never. Never needed to."

"But you said you never won. How could you win if you didn't buy a ticket?"

He flashed a look of mild annoyance, like I didn't understand something very simple.

"That's hardly the point. There are a hundred reasons I've never won anything, and not playing is hardly the point. The point is that I've never won, and the reason is that we've never been lucky as a family. I've never been lucky, anyway. Have you? Have you ever won anything?"

I thought about it. "No, I don't think so."

"What more do you need? We've never won anything."

"Mike won that dollhouse for Gwynn at the church fair. It was pretty big. It was huge. We still have it."

He was looking at me, all puzzled. "A dollhouse? I'm talking about a goddamn CADILLAC here. Winning a dollhouse isn't lucky; no one wants one of those. But everyone wants that car. Especially those people. Look at them. They don't know I'm going to win it. We should get out right now and let them know the show is over and I'm winning."

I'd heard this line of argument often with him. Since I could talk, and likely long before, Joe had sat me down to tell me stories of old Ireland. They were about warriors and kings and great battles and heroes like Cú Chulainn and tyrants and evil dark-hearted bastards like Cromwell. The bastards eventually stole victory from the Irish, every time. The Irish were smarter and braver and had God on their side, but somehow, the English sons-of-bitches with their conniving and their politics always carried the day, and the Irish were handed another glorious defeat. There were so many, and he never tired of talking of them.

In his stories, we were always the best, but always the losers, too. He liked it that way, the nobility of never surrendering and suffering a loss for the good fight. I wonder though, as he sat on the deck of his big house and looked out on his big cars and his big family, was he ever heartbroken at having won? He had it all, and I think part of him would have been happier to have a real grudge against the world, rather than to be sitting in a Cadillac imagining his misfortune.

He sat there, smiling out at all the grannies who'd never be driving the one parked in front of the church. "Cars were the reason we came to this country, son."

I thought about it and asked him, "Couldn't you say you won by just getting here? Not everyone could get here and you love it here. That's a kind of winning. Like winning the world lottery."

"I guess so. So, do we have a bet?"

"About what?"

"I bet you I win that car. I bet you that when the old padre in his big stained outfit gets up in the church hall to announce the winner, that the name he gives is Joe Nolan. What say you?"

"What are we betting?"

"Ice cream at Hoffman's."

"I have to pay for it?"

"Of course not. But you'll have to live with losing, and you'll weep with anger when you see me in that there shiny Cadillac driving around, with old ladies calling me Joe the Winner. That's punishment enough."

"OK."

You had to hand it to a man who could be over the age of seventy and still thrilled at the possibility of winning a car he didn't even remotely need and being able to rub the victory in his grandson's face.

"You'll regret this one," he said.

"Why?"

"I've an in with the Big Man."

"Can we get some ice cream now?"

"You paying?"

"Oh, please, Grandpa."

"OK."

The summer drifted by the way it does when you're young, and there's no job to be going to, and the dread of the coming school year is somewhat toned down by the fact that you forget to dread it as you're at the beach all day. I mostly forgot about the car raffle, because even Joe could not guarantee victory in a church raffle, no matter how close to God he claimed to be. He wouldn't let anyone forget, though. He told everyone. He mentioned it at the ice cream store. He mentioned it when he went to buy milk. He mentioned it everywhere.

"Have you seen that Cadillac out by the church?" was usually the way he started. Then he'd engage them in his whole conversation about how he'd never won anything. There was scarcely a person from Point Pleasant to Seaside Heights that didn't know that Joe Nolan had never won anything in his life and that he was going to win that Cadillac.

We were at the beach one day in August, me under a beach towel that I had put over the back of my mom's beach chair on one side to make a little fort. The other side was held down by two pieces of driftwood, which unbeknownst to my family I would carry home with me in the folds of my beach towel to squirrel away in the attic. I had an entire driftwood collection no one knew about. I was fascinated with the stuff, but could think of no practical purpose for it. You couldn't even really display much of it in your room, Kathy had seen to that. It fell under the category "crap" in her book. So I hid it away in hopes that I would eventually discover a use for it, perhaps when I took up whittling in my old age.

The ocean was full of jellyfish at that time of the year, so I wasn't in the water. I burned easily in the sunlight, so I'd built my fort for protection, but also so I could read without being bothered. It amazes me how comfortable people feel in disturbing you when you're reading. "What are you reading there?" they say. Well, nothing now. Now I'm talking to you.

The peace of the afternoon was cut short by gigantic laughter and the sounds of people talking excitedly. I'd barely looked up from my book when I heard my name called. I emerged from my hiding spot and a group of people were all gathered around the Fifth Avenue beach entrance, smiling and laughing. Kathy was waving me over, so I put my book down and put on my T-shirt and hat so as not to be burned. I ran up to the group and saw Joe emerging from the scrum wearing a Hawaiian shirt and a straw hat and white patent leather shoes and a huge smile. He was guffawing and people were laughing with him. It was all people from the neighborhood who knew us. They got a little quieter as I walked up. Joe looked around at them.

"Who wants a ride in Joe Nolan's brand new Cadillac, eh?"

Oh, jeez, I thought. It was Sunday. It was August. The raffle. They all pretended to go wild, like it was the best thing in the world, laughing with him. Cries of "Me, Joe!" rang out.

He looked around at them and threw the keys to me. I caught them and looked down at them shining in my hand. When I looked up at him, I realized everyone was quiet and looking down at all three and a half feet of me. Once again he'd made me the center of attention.

"I owe you an ice cream," I said. Everybody laughed at that.

"Yes, you do. An ice cream for the Big Winner." Everybody followed us up to the road. There, parked so it practically blocked the
entrance, was the big gleaming Cadillac. It still had the sign for the
raffle in the window, and I had no doubt it would stay there for some
time, until the Big Winner was satisfied everyone had seen that his
long streak of losing and misery had finally been broken. My mother
handed me ten dollars and told me to buy Joe an ice cream and bring
some back for my sisters. We got in to the mock cheering of the neighborhood as Joe and I waved at them like Miss America pulling away.

He was laughing and with a wave of his hat out the window we
pulled onto Route 35. "Great, isn't it?" He smiled broadly as we ca-
reened down the road, breaking the speed limit in leisurely fashion as
we cruised towards Point Pleasant. He held his head high, occasionally
looking across the new dashboard and patting it.

"They love it," I said.

"They should, it cost me enough."

"What did?"

"The raffle."

"What do you mean?"

"Winning doesn't come cheap in the Catholic Church, son."

"Oh."

I looked around the car, admiring the big leather seats and playing
with the windows. A thought occurred to me. "You mean the tickets
were expensive?"

"Well, I guess. Ten dollars apiece."

"Uh-huh." I could see he was looking over at me and trying to stop
from exploding with laughter. "How many did you buy?"

"All of them, I think." And that was it. He devolved into guffawing, slapping the dashboard of the car and the seat in between. "Yes,
yes, damn near every one of them."

"You're kidding!"

"I am not. I went and gave the Father So-and-So a check and asked
how many tickets there would be in the raffle, and I bought about half
of them. I liked my odds. I figured I could have gone and bought them
all but that would mean I cheated. So I just bought enough that I'd be
able to tell if I really won or not, and I did. I won it.'

"Jeez."

"Yeah, great isn't it? I WON. Everybody made out. We got the car, the padre gets the money, and the old folks get to hate Joe Nolan for a year because he made losers out of them. Tell me something. Would you want the car, if I could give it to you?"

"Sure. But I'm only eight."

"That's hardly the point. Well, maybe it is. OK, well, I can't give you the car, but how about I pay for all the ice cream and you keep the money your mother gave you?"

"That works."

"Good." We pulled in to the ice cream place, and there were families all around, eating their cones and laughing. We sat there a minute in the car. Joe was never one for leaping out of a car like a cop when he pulled up. He usually had to adjust his glasses and make sure his hair was perfect, the Elvis man that he was.

"So we'll get rid of the old Caddy then?" I said.

"Why?"

"Do you need two of them?"

"Nah. I'm going to get rid of this one."

"Why?"

"I'm giving it to the priest."

"I don't get it. You wanted it all summer, and you paid all kinds of money for it."

"I didn't really want it, though."

"You said you did."

"For a laugh, you know—give people something to talk about and a reason to give the padre a bunch of dough."

"He'll only spend it on getting more people to bother God."

He laughed. "I suppose so. But he's a nice man, and I don't think he ever had a car like that."

"So it's a good thing, then?"

"Yeah, buying something for someone who can't buy it themselves is pretty good."

"Thanks for offering me the car, by the way. I'll get one eventually."

He looked around the car and out the windows at the kids jumping

up and down in the parking lot, spilling ice cream all over themselves, and was suddenly quiet. He sat a second, and I sat with him.
It was good to know when to be quiet around him. It meant he was
thinking.

He turned to me. "If you ever really want something, don't ever
tell anybody. Not even me, your best good pal. Keep it to yourself,
right? It's important to want things. But keep it to yourself . . . keep
it like a secret."

"OK." I knew this was one of those things he meant to be taken
seriously. "OK, I will."

"That way, if you don't get it, no one can ever laugh at you or feel
bad for you for not having got it. And if you get it . . . well, it's yours
alone, isn't it?"

"Yes."

"Good man. OK, then," he said, getting out of the car. "Let's make
sure we spill ice cream on the seats so the padre doesn't go asking for
a Mercedes next, all right?"

Chapter 11

PLENTY IS NEVER ENOUGH

From what I hear, all I did was work. Can that really be all I did?

You rode bikes, too.

Jerk. Did any of this at least rub off on you?

Oh yeah. And from an early age. Some kids wanted to be astronauts and firefighters. I am not shitting you when I say that from the age of five I wanted a desk job. Now I'm living the dream.

Congratulations.

It didn't start out that way, I can promise you.

B ob Dylan said that in New Jersey anything's legal as long as you don't get caught, and that's just about right. Mike knew that work had made him, and it was going to goddamn well make you, too.

I was twelve and I told Mike that I needed a job because I needed money. This was not entirely true, but it wasn't a lie either, although my expenses boiled down to comic books and Coca-Cola. There was the possibility that a job could put more of both within reach. More to the point was how bored I was in the summer—my parents would rent a house from Joe and would naturally expect you to go up to the beach and enjoy it. But I didn't enjoy it. Everyone was sweating and covered in oil, the sand was hot and the sun was bright, and to this day, I can never really figure out why that is a good thing.

So a job seemed like something that might show a little initiative and at least get me paid for being inside. The problem was, I was only twelve, and beyond mowing lawns, there wasn't much I could do legally. In New Jersey, this is almost never a problem.

Joe Nolan had a revolving list of people who he had helped out, or had done favors for, or who just plain liked him and would do anything for him. So when Mike called him and told him I needed a summer job at the beach, it was done. He walked into the porch where I sat surrounded by comic books and told me that the old man was coming by tomorrow to get me a job. I asked what I'd be doing, and he laughed. "If I had to guess, I'd say something involving a cash business." At the time, I had no idea what this meant or why it was funny.

Joe came by the next day. I instinctively walked outside and started to get in the car. "Not today, little man. We can walk to this place."

We walked down the street together, Joe doing his usual comic bit of taking his hat off to people saying hello and waving at everyone like he was running for office. He even waved at the surfer guys who were too cool to look at anything, and they waved back thinking he must be someone they should know. He said to me, "Are you good with your hands?" I didn't know. "Well, you will be soon, or you'll be losing them. Be careful in this place, and make sure you act like a good kid. I've known this guy forever."

Five blocks away and we were at what everyone in town referred to simply as "the market." It was your basic general store, only with a few characteristics unique to the Jersey Shore: it was open every day from May to September, prices were incredibly high and service was incredibly low. It was a typical beach market—five aisles of essentials, a fruit and vegetable stand, and a deli in the back. There were teenage boys staffing the deli, and teenage girls at the registers up front. The place smelled of salt, old vegetables and newspapers, and there were old people standing in the aisles holding jars of pickles and staring at them for no apparent reason.

Milling about the place were people who had come down for the day or the week with their kids, not knowing or not caring that they were going to be fleeced mightily and righteously by the local retail merchants as punishment for only coming down in the summer. There was a twenty percent markup across the board, even for the papers.

It might say one dollar on the front of the *Times*, but brother, you are taking out another quarter to read the news today. A gallon of milk was like liquid gold in this place. You could not have your Entenmann's chocolate donuts without it, and they knew it. So they got you coming and going.

We walked straight into the back. Sitting at an improvised desk made out of a card table and a chair which had "St. Joseph's By the Sea, Grade Six" written on the back of it was a man who looked to be in his sixties in khaki workmen's pants, a hideous Izod shirt with awful greens and blues and an ancient pair of sneakers. Naturally, he wore dark socks which slumped down into the sneakers so you could see mostly leg. He looked not unlike a more wrinkly Ronald Reagan with his dyed black hair. His skin was ghost white, and you got the feeling he didn't leave this room very often.

"Son," said Joe, "this is George. George, this is my boy I told you about."

"Well," George boomed. He turned in his chair. "What's this all about? Had enough of the waves and the little girls?" It was easy to tell he didn't like people very much, and easier still to tell that he didn't really consider kids to be people anyway.

"That's right," I said.

George smiled and looked up at Joe. "OK, son. Joe says you want a job, you got the job. How's that?" It was that easy. I had the job. It ruined me for years, as I came to think that all you really had to do to get a job was go in and ask someone. They didn't seem that hard to come by, having pulled it off at the age of twelve in all of thirty seconds.

Joe gave me a look that said well done and then left me to George. I heard them just outside the door in the parking lot. "That's all right, then, Joe. I'll take care of him."

George came back into the store and stood with hands on hips. "Son, what do you know about meats and cheeses?" I was unprepared for the pop quiz and stood there looking dumb. He waved me out into the deli, where the guys were busy measuring cold cuts and making sandwiches. They worked on massive slicers with big circular blades. They looked medieval. "This is Bob. Bob, you're going to show young Sean here how to do the job. Son, are you afraid of sharp things?"

"Yes," I said. This was quite true. I was transfixed by the giant blade, picturing a succession of my fingers being added to some old lady's tuna on rye.

"You should be. Don't fucking cut yourself on these. It'll hurt." With this sage advice, he walked back to his office. I was surprised to find I'd be working the slicers. I thought I would have been sweeping up or stocking shelves. There was also the point of law which said that you had to be eighteen to operate the things, and that was a long way away for me.

Bob was a greasy seventeen years old and a total fuck-up. He had a bunch of earrings in his ears. Not one or two, but about ten. He bitched about everything. He told me to watch him and just learn by what he did. Apparently, this meant that whenever I finished making a sandwich, I should say, "Choke on it, you fat fuck," or "I'll show you the meats, you old bitch." It did not take long to figure out that Bob was a pretty bitter dude all around and not really going much further in life than a few exits away from where he'd been born.

I sat on the counter or grabbed stuff from the freezer for him. He acted like he was showing me the world. "You gotta know the difference between the hams, man. The hams will totally fuck you up." There were two kinds of ham. "Cheeses, bro? Don't even get me started, man. That's some veteran shit for you right there." There were three kinds of cheese.

With Bob's capable guidance, it didn't take me long to learn the ins and outs of the place.

Bob talked about his car a lot. It was a real piece of shit, but he talked all day about the tail he got because of it. I could only imagine said tail, given the unbelievably bad shape his Subaru was in. He would come in wearing sunglasses, as if he had been so wasted the night before that he needed them to shield his eyes from the harsh fluorescence. George would tell him to take them off, and then he would start in. "Ohh, yeah. Last night was killer, maaaaan. Fuckin' killer. Got wasted at my old man's house, poundin' Buds. Went to this party down in Seaside, there was all this tail from up north, oh, man. So much tail."

Jack was the other guy who worked there. He was about forty-five and hated everybody, but hated Bob more than anyone. He had been in the Navy and claimed he was a total psycho by saying things like, "I was in the Navy, guy. I'm a total psycho."

"Aye, hey Bob. Bob, hey man."

Bob would still be doing his "I'm so wasted, I banged so much tail" thing for me, and he'd turn and say "Yeah?"

"Shut the fuck up, OK, pal? That's great. Shut the fuck up. Thanks."

Bob would mutter, "Jeez," and then shut the fuck up. I could never tell Jack I liked him, but I did. He was crazy but crazy in a very predictable way. You could just count on him to say the worst thing that came into his head, and as long as you were all right with that, you were all right with Jack.

He'd be done with his shift, and George would say, "See ya tomorrow," and Jack would say, "Sure thing, there, big guy, unless they find me hanging by the neck from a ceiling fan, right? OK, that's great, I'll see ya."

George would shake his head and say, "Seek help, Jack. Real soon."

Jack wore his hair slicked back. He was pale like George, but in an Irish way, not some clammy unhealthy way. He stood with his arms folded, leaning against the counter chewing gum, not looking one bit welcoming. When there were no customers around, he would say things to himself like, "OK, grandma, here's your half pound of turkey breast. How 'bout I take you home and gut you like a fucking turkey, you fucked up old broad? Yeah, shit, you'd like that, you crazy old bird. That's right, old Jack takes you home, I'll dress you up nice. That's good stuff." He'd smile all crazy at you and you'd both laugh.

After my first day, I tried to say goodbye to him, something like, "OK, see ya, Jack." Jack looked up and stuck his chin out: "OK, tough guy, aye, come here, listen, you going home? Yeah? Hope you die. OK? Really, honestly. I mean it. You're a good kid. Hope you die. Have a nice night, hey, why not, right? OK, that's great."

That night when I got home and came through the door, Kathy asked me how it was, and I told her I thought the working life was for me.

The next day, I met Danny. Danny was the fruits and vegetables guy; he was only there on Fridays and Saturdays. He was about five feet tall, Italian, and about a hundred years old. He could barely walk, and when he did, he was all stooped over. He sat on a milk carton next to the fruits and vegetables, and customers couldn't pick their own, he did it for them, smoking a big dirty cigar the whole time. He was a pioneer in the field of sexual harassment.

A lady would walk up and be checking out the apples, and he would say, "Oh, yeah," in his gravelly voice, "these are nice and red and juicy, just like that sweet bottom of yours." Or, "Look at these melons, nice and big, just the way Danny likes them," and wink, before laughing his old man "Ha, ha, ha" laugh and playing with his cigar. None of the ladies ever seemed to mind it. I think he'd been around so long that he was just accepted as the local color, and no one gave a shit.

Whenever the young girls spoke to him, he'd talk to them all day. But if Bob or I wanted to talk to him, he'd cup a hand to his ear and say, "Whaaaaaaaaat? Whaaaaaaaaaat? I can't hear." I knew he liked me at the end of the summer when he gave me a tomato and told me, "Take that home to your mother." George saw it and told me, "That's the big time, bucko. Danny fucking hates you kids. He gave you a tomato, though. That's his heart. Boy, he loves his produce. Sure does."

Danny was so damn old that he had no sense of taste anymore. George made us make him a sandwich every day, so Jack and I would put together the most disgusting combinations you could think of. The foulness of the sandwich varied, but olive loaf was always involved, along with liverwurst and onions. Danny would amble over for his sandwich, and Jack would be waiting, holding it on the counter for him.

"There you go, you fucked-up old geezer. There's your fucking sandwich. Eat up while it's good 'cause it's making me sick back here."

Danny would scrunch up his face at Jack and say, "You're a lousy man. You make shitty sandwiches. No one likes you."

"That's right, you wrinkly old fuck—hey—don't choke on that! Don't choke on it 'cause you'll break little Jacky's heart."

Danny would give him the finger, and they'd both smile. It was all a big game, anyway. "That's right, Yoda—walk away. Chew it twenty times to get the benefit." Then he'd turn to me. "If I ever get like that, shoot me. Seriously, I wanna die before I look like that retarded midget."

George barely noticed any of the shenanigans among the employees. His office was in the back, and that was where he spent most of his time. Occasionally, he'd come out to yell about something, but that was infrequent. I learned a lot about food from him, but mostly I learned that the people serving you probably hated you, and most of them didn't care if what they sold you made you sick or not.

George was the best boss I ever had. He was the P.T. Barnum of food retail. In the mornings, we'd come in and "turn the salads." That meant you'd take a metal spoon and mush the macaroni, tuna and egg salads until the green film that had collected on them overnight was gone. Then you'd spray water on the vegetables on Danny's stand to make them look fresh, even though Danny only came in weekly, so by Thursday, they weren't looking so good. You'd carefully turn the produce so that the bad parts were covered up and the unsuspecting would be sure to take home something rotten. It was evil, but it was also minimum wage.

Every month or so, the health inspector would come by. The first time I heard that the health inspector was coming, I was worried about my age and I told Jack about it. Jack laughed his crazy laugh and waved his hand at me.

"Listen, there, little man, all right. Some government fat cat comes in here, tries to tell us how to do business, we kick him in the head, OK, chief? Bust his ass into the back and throw him on the spit with the chickens, huh? How 'bout that? That's good shit, right there. How you like that, there, conquistador, huh? You like that, sure, you like that. That's good, that's the plan."

So Jack was no help. I stayed worried until I saw the guy. Joe would have called him "a real piece of trash," and he was. You could see this guy was just a total degenerate. He shuffled his way into the store, and from his hangdog look, you could tell that when he wasn't at the track, he was pretty much at the bar. He asked for George at the counter, and Bob went and got him.

George came out smiling, and they shook hands. George clapped him on the back, and they went in the back room, leaving me with Jack, who stood leaning against the counter with a huge smile across his face that said he knew all kinds of things you didn't know.

"See that? You worried about that? What'd I tell ya, huh? This guy, he's a first class piece of shit and we own him, right? Nothing to worry about, no reason to shoot this guy—HEY, hold your fire, that's right, save it for later. Bang, Jacky's got you covered, BANG!" and then he clapped his hands and retied his apron.

When I went back and forth to get more bags and rolls, I could see that they were sitting in the back with their legs up on the card table, playing poker, and there was a big bottle of Jack Daniel's open in front of them. On nights when the health inspector would be there, George's wife would come and get him. I've no idea how the inspector made it back to the track, but the filthy sack of shit was always in there like clockwork every month. It got to where I didn't even hide from him anymore.

We were all paid under the table in cash. It worked out great for everybody. At the end of the week, you'd go in the backroom with George, and he'd give you the envelope with the cash in it. My second week there, he told me I was doing a great job, and that he was happy he'd hired me. It was a great feeling and I felt like a millionaire. I even bought my sisters each a candy bar at the 5&10 on the way home, entering the house like a junior Mafioso after his first hit and throwing cash around. Kathy would confess to being a little worried by how much I enjoyed showing up at work, but the truth was I just didn't mind hanging out with Jacky and the boys.

I loved the feeling of having money in my pocket. I understood a little better why my old man busted his ass so hard after that summer. I'd work overtime in the place and show up early, because George was good to me, and Joe liked him. I barely had anything to spend any money on, so I got a bank account and put it in there. But I kept most of it in my pocket so I could flash the green like Joe did.

Jacky would ask me why I kept so much dough on me. Why didn't I keep it in a bank, a little guy like me, I should be holding on to my dough.

"Cash is king," I told him.

Jacky smiled. "You fucking A it is, kid."

So that's how I learned what working was like in New Jersey. Lots of degenerates, a little dishonesty, and you should know someone to get a piece of it.

Chapter 12

LIFE WITH THE LIONS

It wasn't all roses, though, old man. With the job Joe got me, I was happy. Then you had to get involved.

Naturally. Let me guess, I put you together with some asshole.

Did you ever. It still turned out to be a good thing. What they used to call "a good little lesson" on the basketball team. A good little lesson meant someone usually knocked you on your ass a bit.

And then cameth the summer of Rocky. Mike suggested I get a job with a guy he knew working construction for the summer. It paid better than making sandwiches, and I'd been up and down the strip, looking for a better job.

"None of us ever knew how to fix anything," he said. "Think of it as self-improvement."

The first time I was introduced to Rocky, it was through a client of Mike's, a sunglasses and polo shirt-wearing guy named Scott. This guy owned a small construction firm, and my old man had talked to him about me coming around and helping out during the summer. Mike had had enough of the cushy jobs Joe had found for me behind sandwich counters.

"How would you feel about working construction this summer?" he'd said. He strode into my room with a swagger, as if he'd just been out building something himself.

"Not sure. I've never really done anything like that."

"Well, maybe it's time you learned how to do a few things." He said this with total confidence, like he'd worked at a hardware store all his life and was now welcoming me into the fold.

"But none of us know how to do anything."

"I have an entire workbench full of tools." True, he did have one. The tools were all brand new. They would remain brand new forever, as they would never see the light of day. The man had not done anything beyond hanging a picture in my entire life.

It would be useless to point this out. I could see I was being offered a job, and I didn't have anything else lined up. "OK."

I remained skeptical about Mike's latest attempt at self-actualization on my behalf. This was a man known throughout our neighborhood for a little stunt he pulled a few years back. We were having a Christmas party, and the path to our front door was packed with ice. I stood out there pathetically chipping away at it for hours until the old man realized there was no way I was going to even make a dent in it. He hollered at me to step aside and emerged from the garage with a gas can and a lighter. He proceeded to douse the entire path in gasoline and light it ablaze. This was witnessed by neighbors, and while effective after several dousings, became the stuff of local legend, proof of the old man's rigid insanity.

I arrived my first day, and the nervousness I'd felt before going was entirely justified. I'd been told just to show up on the site and speak to "Rocky." I'd pictured a hulking, sweaty guy with long hair and tattoos who looked like he was just waiting to kick my ass and who'd likely been in prison. I was relieved to find that he was indeed all of those things. I walked up to the site at eight a.m., and they were just unloading a big van full of tools. There were four guys, already sweating and looking pissed off. I approached the least badass looking of them.

"Hi, I was looking for Rocky."

The guy looked at me. "Well, did you find him? Back when you were looking for him?"

"I mean, I am looking for him."

"That's him, there. The big fat ugly guy. Enjoy."

"Him there" had '80s-band hair down past his shoulders and tattoos everywhere. This was back when having tattoos counted for something. These weren't tribal or anything close to it, this wasn't fratboys from Stonybrook at Seaside Heights, these were the kind of tattoos you only get in jail.

"Hi, Rocky?"

"Yeah." He gave me a quizzical look, and then, like he was waking up, he knew who I was. I would come to find out that he did this all of the time, giving you a confused look and then suddenly managing to get it. "You're that kid Scott said would be here."

"Yeah."

"OK. Well?"

"Well? What should I do?"

"What can you do?"

Nothing he could have asked would have been worse than that. The only truthful answer was, "Nothing." I mean, literally nothing. I came from a family that called a plumber when there was hair in the sink. If the lights went off because of a blown fuse, we were instantly back in the Dark Ages. I had seen my father beat a toilet bowl with a plunger like a caveman when it refused to stop overflowing, because he did not know how to turn the valve off, all the time yelling, "Motherfucking shitter! You motherfucking shitter shit fuck!" while he beat it.

I was at worst a minor disaster and at best an occasional annoyance from the start. They asked me to cut some lengths of wood on a big band saw. I could see them looking at me, waiting for a finger to go flying. Clearly, they were unaware of my time spent making sandwiches. I was a pro around sharp objects. That wasn't the problem. The problem was that I didn't know that when you measured wood, you needed to leave space in your measurement for the part that you'd sawn off. So everything I cut turned out to be too short by about a quarter of an inch.

Rocky wasn't pissed, though. He was confused. He was always a bit confused. "How did you not know that?" he said with a look on his face like he'd caught me fucking a watermelon.

"I just never did this before. I'll go redo it."

"Nah, don't bother. Jack will handle it. Why don't you just look in the truck and find me the Cedar Stretcher?"

"Sure. What's it look like?" He proceeded to describe this tool for me in great detail: it was long, it was metal, probably green, Black & Decker made it.

I went out to the truck and examined the shelves and all the tools lying on the floor. Conscious that I had just been exposed as totally unfit for the job, I wanted to make it up to him and return on the hop, but for the life of me, I couldn't find anything resembling what he described. Dejected, I walked back in and told him I didn't think it was there.

"Really?" he said. "Hey, Jackie, did you leave the Cedar Stretcher in the truck?"

"Of course, Rock. That's always where I put it."

Rocky put his hand to his chin. "Well, kid, it has to be in there. Take another look. We really need it today. Lots of stuff to stretch."

I went back down and must have turned over every nut, bolt and hammer looking for this thing. I tried to think of what it could be used for, how big it would be, where I would have put it if I was them. But there was nothing. I didn't want to go back up, having gone oh-for-two in terms of Jobs Well Done.

But I did. I told him there was nothing there that resembled it. Rocky rose to his full height of five foot two and gave me his vacant, uncomprehending look. "Kid," he said. "Do you really think there is anything in this goddamn world that stretches out cedar?"

"Well . . ." The guffawing from the other guys began immediately. That day earned me the nickname "Greenhorn," not only because that's what they called everybody new, but because I was easily the dumbest new guy ever. I knew this without asking, because the guys would say things like, "Boy, for a rich kid, you got brains made of shit."

Rock talked that day at lunch about prison. I can't remember how it came up, but there we were sitting outside by the bay, and he was talking about how he'd gone up a few times. "But that was all in Pennsylvania," he said. "I'm clean in Jersey."

The best way to earn points with this crew was to bust your ass and I tried, but I was just so damn bad at the job. Everything I touched was a miniature disaster. This was far from the world of sandwich making, a world I at least understood in a vague way, as I enjoyed sandwiches. Construction was another world to me. I had never so much as built a model airplane. I was deaf in one ear, and my hands shook. I was a total embarrassment.

I learned new phrases from the crew. Anyone who hassled them or created the least bit of hassle was referred to only as "fucking guy."

"Did you hear what this prick wants done to his kitchen? Rip the entire thing out from top to bottom? Those counters can't be more than five years old. *Fucking guy.*"

"Barry called to tell Scott that he's too messed up to come in today. You believe this *fucking guy?*"

James was the other fucking guy I got to know well. He flat out looked like a pirate. One eye was all glassy and weird, and he had scars on his face. He also wore a Little Steven–type bandana on his head and shorts that resembled David Banner's once he'd finished Hulking out. He was usually shirtless anyway. He liked to surf. I'd see him at all the bars, and rare was the day when he didn't show up and inform us, "I've got a massive fucking hangover. Don't talk to me. Seriously. No one fucking talk to me." I've no doubt he would absolutely kill someone if they crossed him, but he was great to me.

These guys were nuts. They'd fire nail guns at one another, throw hammers, take shits in people's toilets when they weren't supposed to. We'd be replacing a window at some old lady's house, and not only would she have to pay for the window and the labor, she'd come home to the smell of two guys having dropped about three bombs each in her bathroom. These guys didn't get the job done quickly, either. They'd be in the can for half an hour, and the courtesy flush was totally unheard of. They'd just be in there reading the sports page, or even worse, smoking. Imagine coming home and your nice bathroom with the pink towels and the flowered wallpaper smells like hangover shit and cigarettes.

The long-held image of the construction worker whistling at hot women as they walk by held fast with these guys. They'd do it from rooftops while replacing shingles. They'd stop what they were doing inside the house to lean out the window and yell, "Hey, baby!" or just whistle.

At no point did they think that the girl was going to walk up the driveway and ask them out. I don't really know what they were thinking. The closest I can come is to take the anthropological view and just say that it has always been done.

I did ask about it once. I'd been on the site for about a month, and I said to James, "What's the deal with the hollering at chicks?"

He reflected a bit. "Well, you just can't let them walk by unharassed, you know? They gotta know we're watching."

I spent the rest of the first day hammering nails in. Scott drove me home and said he'd talked to the guys and gotten a full report. "'Greenhorn,' huh? You should probably get to like that name."

"Yeah, it's fine. My lacrosse coach calls me worse."

He raised an eyebrow. "You might not want to mention your lacrosse coach around the guys. They'll think you're a fag."

"Right, got it.'

Mike was outside when we pulled up to the house. We walked over, and he asked Scott how I'd done on my first day. Scott was only too truthful.

"He hammers like a woman."

Mike's face darkened a bit. He looked at me. "How can that be? We hammer around here . . . you know . . . all the time."

I let that face-saving lie stand and said, "I have a lot to learn," before I walked inside.

Rocky and I got sent to do a job together one day in July. It was hot. We had to replace the floors and some beams underneath some guy's dining room. By now, these guys had decided I wasn't such a massive boob. I was good for shoveling and breaking things. I was quiet, and I didn't tire easily, and after that first day, I'd started picking a lot of things up. I worked hard, and was getting better quickly.

We sawed through the floor and ripped all kinds of stuff out. We talked about football, what his tattoos meant, and what my old man did. Now, these guys would drink on the job from time to time. A few of them would smoke weed, and usually that all started in the early to late afternoon. As the week went by, it got earlier and earlier, until Friday rolled around and they were at it by lunchtime. The idea of these men operating massive power tools in this state should have scared me, but they were generally a docile bunch.

About midway through the job, Rocky opened the refrigerator and found two six-packs of Heineken. "Fucking excellent," he said. I was knee-deep into the kitchen floor, standing on a mix of dirt and sand. "You want one?" he asked.

"Nah, that's OK. Thanks."

"Right." Rocky cracked one open with his teeth. Throughout the afternoon, he kept opening them. He went through all twelve by the time the day was over. His eyes were good and glassy, but other than that, not much else about him had changed. He was an excellently functional drunk, and it was a pleasure to watch him work. He gave me a ride home and thanked me for putting in a good day, and I expected never to hear of the job again.

Two weeks later, Scott pulled up to the house we were working on. I was up on the second floor, and I looked out to see a dejected-looking Rocky getting out of the passenger seat. Scott looked pissed. He was waving his arms around and talking to James. James had a great Crazy Eye, and he was staring Scott down with it, until finally Scott threw his hands up and said, "Fuck it, I'll find him myself."

Five seconds later, I heard him bellowing from downstairs, "Sean! Sean! Where are you?" I walked downstairs, and there was the whole crew and Scott standing in the living room of the house. They were all looking at me, and it was clear they knew something I didn't know. Scott said, "Come on, we need to talk." As I walked past the guys, I saw a look on their faces that I had not seen since Sister Joan had dragged Chuck Gigante out of the classroom down to the principal's office. The penguins were on to him for knowledge relating to stink bombs being set off in the boys' locker room. We all knew who had done the job, and that knowledge, in the eyes of a nun, made you just as guilty as the guy who set it off if you didn't tell.

I remembered the look on the faces of the other guys in class as

Chuck was dragged down the aisle by one ear. I saw it on the faces of
the rest of the guys in the crew again as I walked out with Scott. It
was a heavy, scared look that said, "Are you a rat? Are you going to rat
us out? Remember your friends."

I got into Scott's car, and we drove the few short blocks to his
house on the bay side of the island. We got out, and he gestured towards the front door. I walked in and was consumed by the icy blast
of air conditioning. It was enough that in a few minutes, I would be
legitimately cold.

"Have a seat," he said. I sat down on a wicker chair, feeling that I'd
be less likely to get that dirty than I would with one of his old lady's
expensive couches. Scott took a couch.

"Well?" he said.

"Well?" I said.

"I think you know why we're here." I didn't really.

"No."

"The beers, Sean. We're here because of the beers in Mr. Jackson's
house. I want you to tell me the truth about what happened. Rocky
is denying the whole thing, and I know he's lying." What a fool. This
guy just told me what Rocky's story was without me even having to
try and figure it out. I wanted to tell him what a horrible nun he'd
have made.

Instead, I told him, "Honestly, you're going to have to tell me what
you mean. I don't remember anything like that."

He looked like he had not really expected that. He knew Rocky
took them. He knew I was the only other person there. He knew I
was lying.

"Sean, why is a guy like you lying to protect a guy like Rocky?"

"Don't call me a liar. Seriously, do not." I acted pissed off.

"You were the only other guy there. You were with him all day.
Jackson says when he left, there were beers in the fridge. When he got
back, there weren't. They're just a few beers, so let's not make this a
federal case. Were you there all day?"

"Yeah."

"Was Rocky out of your sight at all?"

"No."

"Did you see him take those beers?"

"No."

"Come on. Nothing bad is going to happen to Rocky. I just want the truth." Now I was pissed off. The nuns had tried this, too— "Nothing will happen to little Johnny if you're honest"—it was an easy thing to believe, but totally untrue. The kid's ass would be red as a barn when they were done with him, and I knew Rock would be fired if I ratted on him, and all for some beer that couldn't have been more than ten dollars.

"Scott, I told you. I saw nothing. My story won't change."

"Fine. I can't say I'm not disappointed about this." I could see he really was. It was clear that he saw us on the same team. He wore khakis and drove a nice car and was a client of my old man's. We were supposed to look out for one another, and what kind of person was I to be taking the other side? I sat there on his wicker chair, and I hated him a little.

He drove me back to the site and mentioned that if I remembered something, I should be sure to tell him. I didn't say anything as I got out of the car. When I walked into the house, Rocky was the first person I saw. He didn't waste any time.

"What did you tell him?"

"About what?"

Rock rolled his eyes. "About the beer."

"Oh. Nothing. I just told him I didn't remember seeing a thing. No idea what happened there." A look of mild surprise crossed his face, and then a slight smile.

"OK. That's good." It was as close to a thank you as I would get. A few of the other guys nodded and looked at one another the way you did when the littlest guy on the baseball team hits a dinger far into right field over the outfielder's head. This wasn't the crowd for hugs and thanks, but at the very least, I had exceeded their expectations. It was only for one day, but easily the most important day for Rocky. I was never called "Greenhorn" again, and the hassle about how bad I sucked at everything went away for good. James still called me "Fuckstick" and "Poonwaste" everyday, but in a way that made me sure he wouldn't club me to death for dropping nails all over while we were on a job.

Mike found out about it from Scott sometime in the weeks after. "I heard about the beer thing. Scott doesn't want you back next year."

"I thought he wouldn't."

He took his glasses off and set them down on the coffee table. "I'll say this for you. At least you're paying attention. Not that it'll get you anywhere."

Chapter 13

DETAILS OF THE WAR

Uncle Eddie. I remember him. He was my Joe.

That's a good way to put it.

Do you think he missed me when Joe stopped talking to me?

Definitely.

Most people probably grow up thinking their old man is invincible. He's the guy you learn your moves from, he's bigger than you, he shows you how to do everything. When someone is always around, maybe you expect he always will be. We never really did in our house. I used to worry all of the time about how Mike would die. If you asked me for a good reason why, I didn't have one. He just seemed to be the kind of person who would never have to stop, like the Tasmanian Devil spinning around in those old cartoons. You knew the only way he was going to stop was if he crashed into something. I thought all of the time about how he would break in the end. He lived so hard that it seemed a fall could never be far away.

Mike told me that back in the Big War, they let you keep your service weapon if you came home. One had been described to me in some detail, a black .45 brought home in the rucksack of one Lt. Col. Edward Nolan from the war in Europe, a gift to his younger brother Joseph, and a reminder of who went, and who didn't have to. I never saw it. I only heard about it from Mike, never from anyone else.

There were relatively few men who Mike Nolan respected, and fewer who he would ever admit to respecting. Very occasionally, he would mention that somebody or other had "done the right thing" or "been around when it counted." It was about the highest praise he could offer, to have done something that mattered, that produced a few ripples in the Big Pond that carried a few people to shore. That was about it.

Mention Uncle Eddie and it was like asking a priest how he felt about Jesus. Mike would go all quiet, look past you, over your shoulder like he could see for twenty miles, and if you were lucky, tell you about something great that Eddie had done. He had done a thousand great things. Mike would often refer to "my uncle," and he had a few of them, but the only guy he ever meant was Eddie.

In his youth, Eddie had run a street gang in Newark called The White Eagles, which was less of a gang and more of a social society dedicated to emptying bars of undesirables so that his gang of undesirables had more room in empty bars. The gang consisted of the nucleus of the three brothers, Eddie, Jimmy and Joe, and their pals, all of whom were scrappy and prone to yelling, none of whom enjoyed a crowd. They were a relative novelty as far as gangs went. Their big scheme for clearing places out was nothing more than walking inside and beating the crap out of one another. Jimmy would punch Eddie, Eddie would punch Joe, and so on. Soon ten guys no one knew had walked in and begun beating the hell out of one another, and the place would empty. The waiting time for drinks would plunge. When asked why no one ever kicked them out of those bars, Joe looked at you like you were stupid. "We were tough."

They were tough. These guys were men even before they went to war.

When the second war with the Germans came, Eddie and Jimmy joined the Army, and the way Mike told it, Eddie participated in every major landing, fighting through North Africa, Sicily, Italy and then finally landing in France, across Belgium, and on into Germany, before finally taking a dump in Hitler's toilet and calling it a day. His prowess on the battlefield was legendary. He had killed anything that moved or didn't wave our flag to his satisfaction. It was said, he had come home with fresh Nazi blood on his boots. Supposedly, he had also brought home that weapon, his little souvenir for his brother. Maybe part of the reason he gave it away was because he didn't want to look at the damn thing anymore. Anyone could understand that.

His stories were told and retold endlessly. Mike Nolan knew a few, Joe Nolan knew a few, and they would occasionally roll them out for you if you were lucky, usually late at night and usually by way of telling you that anything bad that ever happened to you paled in comparison to what Eddie had been through, up to his neck in mud and blood, eating guts and wrecking cities.

Eddie was impressive when you saw him. He stayed in great shape. Even by the time I got to know him in his sixties, the man was an ox. He had brilliant white hair combed back so that he looked like his head might take off. His shoulders stood straight back like he was always at attention. He had the most prominent of the already fairly prominent noses in the Nolan family. You could split a rock on it, and he stood looking at everyone who passed by at parties like he was St. Peter interviewing people for heaven. He loved to cock a thumb at someone walking by and say to you, "Do you believe this guy?" You shook your head no, vigorously, because if Eddie wasn't having it, there was no goddamn way you were having it either.

Smoke hung around Eddie in a perpetual halo. It circled him, seeming to be everywhere, and I cannot picture him without a cigarette in his hand, gesticulating at someone or something, calling people out, motioning them over for a big hug, laughing a huge laugh.

The place where Eddie and his brother will always live in my head was outside Joe's house, on the deck standing next to the pool, drinks in their hands, shooting the breeze with people at parties. They loved parties. They smiled, they radiated, they took shit from no one. By the time I knew them, they had no more explaining to do. Their wars were won, their cash was made, they didn't clear out the bars, they owned the bars. These were guys who could achieve what they'd always wanted, come out on top, and not sit around feeling guilty about it, or brooding about how the fight was over. To hell with the fight; they loved living.

The three of them, Eddie, Jimmy and Joe, they looked the part, the sons of immigrants who wound up running things. These were the guys who had put the country on the right track, and they had done it in our lifetime. When I was ten years old, looking up at these characters holding court and shaking hands at parties, they were giants. There was nothing they could not do, their balls were made of steel, and they said yes to everything, and most people around them probably wished they were them. I did.

You had to hear any story about Eddie secondhand, because the entire family had been put on notice to never bring up the Big Fight. Bringing it up led to raised eyebrows, reproachful stares, and maybe a sit in the car if you were unlucky. His service was barely mentioned publicly, and it barely had to be. You knew who he was when you walked into a room. There are men like that, guys who always have a circle around them, people that everybody wants to talk to. After a party, on the way home, you knew husbands would turn to wives in the car and say things like, "Did I tell you what Eddie said? That guy, he says the damnedest things."

Occasionally, there would be some fool who mentioned something Eddie didn't care to talk about. There was a woman at a black tie party at Joe's house who approached him while a few of us were standing around bullshitting. I was not bullshitting. I wanted to be standing with the guys who were, hoping someday that I would be invited into the circle of bullshitters, invited to stand at the bar with them, drinking scotch and saying things about my car, or my house, or my old lady.

This lady walked up, swaying a bit, and said, "Is that Eddie, talking about the Army?"

No one said anything. Eddie killed his drink.

"We were talking about the pool."

"Go on, Eddie, tell us about France. I'd love to see France," she giggled. Her husband laughed and took her arm.

"Let's go see that pool, Janey."

"Oh, no,'" she waved him off. "Let's hear about Paris, about marching through Paris and all those boys in foxholes." She continued with the giggling.

"Well," Eddie said. "It was beautiful. A lovely country. Wonderful people."

"Oh, were they?"

"Yes. Wonderful."

"What about those German boys? Were they lovely, too?"

"Welllll . . ."

"Oh, go on, Eddie, tell me something."

His eyebrows came down, he seemed to grow a few inches, and he shook the ice in his glass. "It was tough going, lady. They were probably like us. I hardly ever saw them up close, it was never like that. The only ones you ever saw face to face were either dead or being walked the other way. Prisoners, you understand." She nodded along, as Eddie's eyes turned narrow and his voice grew slow and patient, drawing out each word so that the meaning was completely, horribly clear.

"There wasn't a lot of food sometimes, and most nights we barely slept. We didn't exactly carry tents. Prisoners weren't really an option for us most of the time. We were flying units, moving fast across the land, looking for the Germans. But there was always plenty of ammunition. And sometimes you would come onto some of those German boys, maybe at night, in the forest, with no one around. We would surprise them, they'd stick their hands up. No food for them, you see. No food for us, either. No place for us to stay the night. No place for them, either. No prisoners, if you take my meaning. Just us and those boys in the forest, and no one around to hear what we did to them. And most of the time, that's just the way it goes."

By this time her face had become contorted, listening as Eddie drove her off the track of fun party stories and into a place she hadn't really wanted to hear about.

"Well," she said, and walked away. Eddie turned around to the rest of us and began laughing his big Nolan laugh. He winked. "Think she bought it?"

He had married a girl named Laverne, and there were few women who weren't jealous of her. My mom referred to her as "the movie star," and when you saw her, you knew why. She was built like Marilyn Monroe. The only word that did her justice was glamorous, and she was. She walked around like she owned the place, just like her husband, with one hand on her hip and the other holding a cigarette. Eddie called her things like "babe" and "doll," and he was always putting his arm around her. Sometimes doing the right thing worked out just all right.

When he came home from the war, Eddie went right into the Newark Fire Department with his brother Jimmy. Having two of them in the same place was probably trouble, and they spoke often of "our outfit," as if the department belonged to them. These guys strutted around wherever they went like they could buy the place at any time and fire everyone. The confidence that came off of those guys—I don't know where you get balls like that, but I want some.

When I was about ten, Mike walked into the house with a face on him that said something was terribly wrong. No one would ever ask him anything, so it was left to Mom to do it. He was pacing around the kitchen, opening and closing his briefcase, getting himself all worked up.

"My uncle has cancer," he said. With that, he left the house and went on a three-hour walk on the beach.

The old guy could barely get his head around this. You could tell by the way his eyes searched the room, looking for something. This was outside The Big Plan, he had not prepared for Eddie's mortality, and he was pissed. He smacked the table a few times: goddamn cancer, fucking cancer, you gotta be kidding me cancer, the man has a bulletproof liver, this is fucking bullshit. The phone rang a few times that night, and he took the calls up in his office. At some point he came down to find us sitting on the couch. He handed the phone to Kathy.

"That was my father. Party at his house next weekend. For Eddie. A going away party."

Eddie stopped in Jersey in the middle of what he billed his "Farewell Tour," a drive around the country to see every single Nolan relative and wish them well before he went on his way. The party rivaled anything I was to see in the next three decades of my life. Not even college provided the same kind of insanity. Guys wore tuxes. T-shirts were made with Eddie's likeness and the dates of his farewell tour on the back of it. People jumped into the pool in suits and ties. Full beers were thrown into the bay for some unknown reason. A beer keg found its way into the pool. There was a line to get into the house. Joe made a speech. There was a band, all of them wearing Hawaiian shirts and leis. Eddie sang songs. Joe sang songs. The booze ran like a river, and I sat on a balcony up above it all, watching the madness from on high. There were hundreds of people there. Eddie had rolled up in a Cadillac with an Irish tricolor and the stars and stripes flapping on the front hood, like he was the president. We would never see anything like this again.

Only we would. Eddie lived for twelve more years. Twelve more years of parties, and the farewell bashes became a running joke, a middle finger to death, and Joe would throw one whenever Eddie was in town. In the end, he beat the cancer. He died of a heart attack down in Florida. In Mike's office, there is still a pin pushed into a beat up piece of newspaper up on the wall with the obituary for Lt. Col. Edward Nolan of Vero Beach, Florida.

Chapter 14

HAD A DAD

How does a thing like this happen? How does a guy that great and a guy like me just stop talking to each other forever?

I've spent a long time thinking about that, Mike. Sometimes I think it was because your mother was nuts and just didn't like you. Or maybe she wasn't nuts and you were a bad kid, but you and Mom never mentioned it. Maybe you only saw one side, and because of that, so did I. It escapes me, it really does.

And when we stopped talking, you and him stopped talking?

That's right. That's how it goes.

Really? Why does it go like that?

There was never any time I can remember when I slept through the night. When we were kids, my parents used to make us go to bed much earlier than the rest of the neighborhood, and I could hear the kids over the waves crashing from my bedroom at the beach, down on the corner. Most of them were older than I was, and they'd be out way after midnight, and I'd lie there with the window open, listening to them talk. It was nonsense, but I listened to it anyway, tried to listen to how boys talked to girls and who was best at it. Sometimes I'd rest my head on my hands and press my face up to the screen, damp from condensation or the ocean or both, and try to see if the girls were pretty.

There was a pair of old Chuck Taylor's thrown over the telephone wire on that corner, and I'd look at them and wonder who'd put them there and why. I didn't want to be in bed or even in my room, but I knew I wouldn't go out on the corner even if I was allowed to. Joe

Nolan had said it was important to know where you belonged and where you didn't, and I'd learned that already.

When they were gone, I'd read a book by the light coming in off the street lamp outside. I could have turned on the light, but they'd have only told me to put it out. More importantly, the pretty girls outside would know I was up there looking down on them.

That room smelled unlike any other I've ever been in since, of stained wood and sand and salt air and the old books my grandparents filled it with in the winter. Often I'd choose which books to read along the same way I pick out unknown records: by whether I liked the cover art. Over the course of the summer, I'd start a pile of books and the pendulum would move towards the finished pile all summer, most of them read by streetlight.

There was certainly no reason not to sleep. I was a happy kid, untormented by trauma or genius. It just rarely came to me, and when I'd nod off after hours of reading, I'd wake up curled at the top of the bed under bright sunlight and inch away from it to a darker corner of the room.

Everything ended on a Saturday. There was a kind of joy around our house during any week in which we knew we would be going to Grandpa and Grandma's. Everyone seemed to lighten up a bit, because you knew Saturday would be a day by the pool, which meant loads of Coke and cheeseburgers for us and loads of booze for the adults. It was extremely difficult to go over there and have a bad time. I viewed the place as a kind of clubhouse for us all, because Jeanne and Joe had stocked the place with every imaginable toy and foodstuff anyone might ever want.

The summer before this one, Joe had called me over to him on the deck. "I got the next big thing here." He'd made money in a lot of the things he'd invested in. Rumor had it he owned some sort of patent related to escalators, although no one was foolish enough to ask, lest they be given the famous hand wave, which was his way of showing a conversation was over before it had begun.

"What do you think of these trousers?" He was sporting a pair of blue striped pants, worn along with his usual white patent leather shoes with gold buckles and ridiculous pink polo shirt. The man's shirts tended toward the yellow, the pink, the electric blue—"So they know I still got it." Mom called him "Florida in slow motion," and he was as pastel as a man his age could be without becoming a clown.

"I like them." What could you say? Striped pants, big deal.

"You want a pair?"

"Sure."

He ran into the cabana and came out with about twenty pairs of striped pants, so many they were falling out of his arms. He threw the pile in front of me.

"Put 'em on! These are the next big thing, every son of a bitch across the country will be wearing these things in ten years."

I stared down at the pile of pants at my feet. "Why?"

"They're made of PAPER. Go ahead, pick them up. They're made of paper, how incredible is that?"

I touched a pair. It was obviously paper once you had it in your hand. It crinkled ever so slightly, and my first thought was of this cardboard-like substance against my balls; it had to be a killer unless you were just sitting around. Any type of movement would ensure serious pain before you got far.

The look on my face probably said it all. "I'm not too sure about this one."

"I've heard that before. These are great, you spill something on them, you just throw them out. No dry cleaning. No ironing. Nothing. This is going to be huge money. I'll give you some to take home for your friends. Get everybody wearing this stuff, this is the future."

"Sure."

The day was like so many other days there. You could never have known it would be the last of them. I was fourteen and just starting to think of what I might do with my life. Mike had once mentioned that if I ever went to law school, the three of us might be able to start something someday. Sitting on that deck, you knew you belonged to something a bit bigger than you. You were part of a story that came before you, from Brooklyn and Newark and Mayo, and you were part of something that would go on long after you. I liked looking at Mike and Joe, talking conspiratorially. I imagined that great legal puzzles were being dispatched, because these were important men, they knew things and they knew people and the things they did mattered to other people. To matter, they both used to say, is a great compliment to give to someone.

Jeanne and Joe's house was everything ours was not. You could eat anything and you could go anywhere. Growing up in our house was a pain in the ass, because my mother lived in constant fear of one thing: people dropping in unannounced. To her way of thinking, there were hordes of people out there, and not just one or two, but a basketball-team-sized squad of people, and they were just waiting to swing by the house with no warning. In the eighteen years I spent in that house, not once did anyone ever just drop in, but the possibility was always out there. This led to some odd behavior.

Eating anything was frowned on. Anything you opened required some kind of explanation to my mother, and almost any food you could think of was being saved "for company," as if those people might just show up at our door unannounced and with a severe craving for those Oreos you ate yesterday. There was great stuff in the kitchen, but none of it that you could actually eat. When I went to friends' houses for sleepovers, I was amazed at not only the amount of food on display, but also by the fact that it was actually OK for the people living in that house to consume it without having to lie about it.

In Kathy's house, your room was your room, but only because the rest of the house was basically off-limits. What if someone came by and the place was a mess? The house was always in pristine condition and patrolled around the clock by Kathy. You could move a coffee table book an inch, and ten minutes later, it would be right back where it started. The place was more a museum than a residence, and unauthorized entry to any room in which you could not provide a very good reason for being in was severely discouraged. I would occasionally go and sit on the couch in the family room just to see how long it would take someone to say, "Hey, what the hell are you doing in there? You're messing up the couch!" We were like bums constantly being moved along by the cops.

There were no such rules in Joe Nolan's house. When you stayed there, it was like being at the best hotel you could ever check into. The refrigerator was stocked with all of your favorite food, and you could eat it whenever you wanted. There were toys all over the place. They had every cable channel that was offered, and the TVs were all huge. They had one living room downstairs with a U-shaped couch that you could get lost on, it was so gigantic. They had another one upstairs with its own fridge right next to a La-Z-Boy. These people knew how to live, and that house had everything you could want: Coca-Cola, the people that gave a damn about you, and an old man young enough to believe in things like paper pants.

When you stayed over, you got the full treatment. They had all the magazines you liked, following you as you grew up, all the way from *Ranger Rick* to *Spy* to *Rolling Stone*. They put your towels out on the bed, and Joe always left books he thought I'd like in a stack on the dresser. The best part? You never had to make your bed. You didn't have to do a damn thing. You could sit in your bed eating ice cream and drinking Coke all day long if you wanted. Joe Nolan let everyone know he didn't give a shit.

The argument that ended it all was about a jury. Mike's sister Sue had been on a jury, and at some point Mike mentioned that he didn't agree with the decision. Sue flipped out, probably because that was the closest she was ever going to come to the law.

The blocs fell along the lines of how World War I broke out. Mike attacked Sue. Jeanne attacked Mike. Mike attacked Jeanne. Joe attacked Mike. Jeanne attacked Mike. Pretty soon everyone was yelling, and Mike left the house. The words passed were not kind. It was clear right away that this was a major turning point. The echoes of the screamfest were still ringing off the walls, and I remember thinking, this is bad. This is going to be a tough one to get past.

We stayed for a little while longer, Kathy and my sisters and I, but little was said. Joe looked like he was about to have a heart attack, his face was contorted and he kept clutching and unclutching his napkin. Normally, before we left, he would grab some time with me. We'd talk on the deck out by the bay about where to go next weekend, what was going on in school, what did I think of this thing or that person. He treated me like a man when he talked to me, like a guy who was in The Club. Maybe I still had training wheels on, but the intimation was always clear: "I've built something here and you're part of it now." That's how we talked, like I was part of the Big Story, like I mattered. When we finally left that night, he didn't say anything. No one did, we all filed out, down the path to the driveway and into our car. Mike had walked home.

As we pulled down the street, I started to ask what had happened, but Kathleen was a mile ahead of me. "Look," she said. "They've never liked your father. They've never liked me. They hated that we got married, and none of them ever had any time for Mike. We all got along for you guys, so you'd have them around, and we didn't tell you about it. Now you know. They think he's an asshole. I think he's the best man I've ever met in my life. And that's all you need to know. That's what matters."

When we got back to the house, all was quiet. The house was dark, like it had suddenly been closed up for the winter. As I climbed the stairs to the second floor, I hoped to see him sitting on the couch or maybe at the table, but he was nowhere. Nobody said a word, and my sisters went to their room. Mom sat down at the table and looked out at the street.

"Where do you think he is?" I said.

"Probably down at the courts." There was a lighted basketball court on the other side of the island, near the bay, and sometimes he would go down and shoot baskets at night.

"What should I do?"

She was looking out the window, onto the street. The houses across the way were stained red from the setting sun. "What can you do?" she said, but she didn't say it to me.

At the shore, there are beach bikes. These are not like bikes you see anywhere else. They have huge fat tires, like throwbacks to the 1950s, with big wide handle bars and corny paintjobs. Sometimes, if you are female or unlucky, you are given one with a basket up front. They are always slow, to build up any speed at all requires you to stand up and push hard down on the wheels, and for all the effort, they will barely go any faster.

I was standing up on my bike that night when I rode down to the courts, looking for Mike. He was not at the courts. I stopped at the intersection in front of them. The sun was almost gone over the bay, and the lights were on, but he wasn't there. I rode up to the beach, parking the bike by the big sign over the entrance. I looked up and down, but he wasn't there. Up and down the eight streets that made up our town, I drove all over them, looking for him. For all I knew, he was gone. I went home.

I walked up the creaky wooden stairs to the living room, and they were sitting at the table talking. It was heartbreaking to see him sitting there at the table with her. He did not deserve this. I could not fathom what he could have done growing up for this to have been his life, and I could not imagine that I had missed it for this long. I knew that tomorrow he would get up and go back out to the office and keep moving inevitably through his work, and no one he dealt with outside of the family would ever know how shattered he looked sitting there in front of me. I could not allow it. As my mother waved me away and leaned into him, she took his hand. In the reflection of the streetlights, I saw his eyes fixed on the beach and the ocean beyond the houses across the way, and it felt like he'd been sitting in the dark by himself all night somewhere. I wondered how many nights like that he'd spent growing up, with no one there to take his hand, and I was angry for him. It took more than one night to turn a kid into that.

I walked down to the garage and found my bike without turning on any lights. I opened the back door and slipped the bike quietly out onto the back patio and around the side of the house until I was just below the window where Kathy and Mike were. I thought about him sitting there, and I knew I could make this good again. My bike and I pulled out onto Route 35 and headed north.

There were stars in the sky, and a big half moon hung over the ocean as I pedaled. I drove the bike as fast as I could, past the Corner

Store, past the 5&10, the Pizza Parlor, the bars and the ice cream shops. It was that early part of the evening in the summer where darkness has just fallen, and the kids are still out, and people are just starting to head out for the bars. They were everywhere, and as I rushed past them, I wished that I was just one of them, that everything was all right, that I knew there would be ice cream and bars next weekend in New York, or Point Pleasant, or Cape May or anywhere the Cadillac could take us.

The road got dark outside of town, and I went faster, thinking of what I would say, how I could make it right. I'd found out something I'd never known, that Mike and Joe had never really gotten along, like Mike and I had never really gotten along, only much worse. They were different, but that could be OK. The tires on my bike were fat and slow, and my legs felt leaden from pushing through the dim light of the moon and the sound of the bugs from the trees.

On Joe's street, the houses were quiet. I heard the bay and looked out across it as I approached the house. There were still sails out on the bay, and as moved more slowly down the street towards the light from his garage, it felt hard to breathe. The garage was open, so I went in and parked my bike next to the car. I rubbed the Cadillac hood ornament on the front of it for luck and walked towards the front door. I could see in through the big bay window, and there was a glow from a television filling the room.

My knock at the door brought a flurry of shuffling behind it, and in the back of my mind was a worry that they just wouldn't answer it at all. When it opened, Joe stood in the doorway, unsurprised.

"Come on," he said and waved me in. We walked into the living room, and there was Aunt Sue sitting at the table. She threw down her game of solitaire and started to rant again about what an asshole Mike was. "Suzy, please," Joe said. She glared at us, scooped up her cards and went upstairs.

"How'd you get here?" he said.

"I rode my bike."

"I'll give you a lift home."

"I came here to talk to you."

"We'll talk in the car." Not for the last time, I felt like things were happening that I didn't understand. The house that had been our clubhouse, our place, felt like nowhere now to me. No one wanted me there; I had done the exact wrong thing. I felt foolish for having come there, I was only a kid and everything that happened that day had been decided a long time ago, over my head.

"That's OK." My voice cracked, and my face went red. Momentarily I thought of running out onto the deck, jumping into the bay and trying to swim for it. "I'll just take my bike home."

"No, I'll give you a lift."

"There's no point in a lift. You've already made up your mind. I'm not stupid."

"No, you're not. But you don't know everything. Come on."

We walked out through the living room into the garage, the smell of oil and surf wax heavy in the air. I opened the car door slowly, looking down the hood at the ornament that had been worth nothing at all in the end. There was a dreadful feeling of finality about it all, of decisions made and people and places I'd never be welcome around again. Just then I wanted to walk back into the house and run up to my old room, just to see it one last time. I wanted to run out and jump into the pool and swim around at night time, with the lights on, looking up at the stars over the bar. Later I'd sneak into the house when no one was looking and take a Coca-Cola out of the refrigerator, go up to Joe's old office and sit in the middle of the room surrounded by his old books, reading the first three pages of each one to decide which to take home with me.

None of that was ever going to happen again, and as I pulled the car door closed behind me, I thought about never sitting across from him in the car the way we had before ever again. We were pulling out for the last ride, and it would be the shortest ever.

Ever since I was a kid, my hands shook. I could never hold them steady. They would involuntarily twitch, and I did my best to move things around quickly, so no one would see me try to hold a glass full of anything and wind up spilling it everywhere. I'd hide my homework in class, so no one could see how atrocious my handwriting was. I got in the habit of holding my hands together in my lap, one over the other, pressing on one another to create the illusion of stillness. When

I got into the car that night, I held them together in my lap, but they were already still.

Too late I realized the weight of all the years behind us. They'd kept their secret from me for so long that it was overwhelming to consider all at once. I sat staring out the window at the bay, feeling smaller than at any other time in my life. Now I knew what it meant to lose, to know that you'd had a chance, however small, and to not only have come up short, but to have been completely defeated. I couldn't even talk to him. It was already different. A line had been crossed, and the dead silence of the next twenty years had started to descend.

"What is even happening to us?"

He drove slowly. In the light of the streetlights we slowly passed by, I could see his face, sad and contorted and confused, like mine. It all went by too quickly. Soon we were pulling up onto our street.

"You have to be a fatalist about these things. It's always been like this, you just never knew it."

"This is terrible." I didn't look at him. My face was practically pressed against the window, looking out at the houses slipping by along the street.

"Yes. It's time to be a man about things. It's time to grow up and know how things work."

"Can't we change this?"

He didn't answer until we were nearly at the corner. "No," he whispered.

"So that's it."

"Don't let this be your story. It's got nothing to do with you."

"That's a lie."

"I don't know what to tell you. It's been going on for a long time. It has to end sometime."

"So that's the end? We just don't talk? Nobody talks?"

He shook his head and looked out the window, up to the entrance to the beach, like he was waiting for the explanation for how things were going to be to just come to him so he could explain it to me.

I looked up at it, too, but there was nothing there that hadn't been there before. "Grandpa, I'm going to go now."

"OK, son."

The air outside the car was salty, and I could feel the ocean mist coming up over the dunes. There was a wind carrying it over across the houses, and all around me I could hear the sounds of people having parties, carrying on together, the sound of bottles pouring into glasses, and faint music. I stood on the corner, looking down Fifth Avenue at the cars zipping past on the highway, headed up north to anywhere else but here.

Joe and the Cadillac turned slowly onto Ocean Terrace, and I stood under my streetlight, watching his taillights move slowly down the block. I watched the car and remembered it because I thought I had to. He turned onto 8th Avenue, back towards the highway, and was gone for good.

They couldn't know I'd been out, so I went in the back door and slipped quietly up to the second floor and over to the staircase up to the bedrooms. Everyone was in their rooms.

At the top of the stairs was darkness. A thought stopped me before I ascended. I could tell him. I could go in and tell Mike that I'd tried, I'd gone all the way over there and tried for him, maybe like no one else ever had for him, to make things all right. It was something a man would do, it had taken something to do that, and maybe it would at least make the end of this better for him, that his son knew what it meant, and had gone down swinging.

I climbed the wooden stairs carefully, stepping on the edges so they wouldn't creak. There was a light from under their door and I could hear things. A song I'd heard a hundred times before, the singer sounded like us, his voice was pleading and resigned, and later in the song I knew he would cry out for something he'd lost, and I felt like all that right there, standing there alone. Beyond the song, I could hear two voices, my mother and father, speaking softly to one another like I wasn't used to, they sounded like two lovers in an old black and white movie, not like two kids from Jersey. As I raised my hand to knock on the door, I heard sobbing, great big tearful sobs, like a flood coming out, and I stopped.

The man in the song was right, the darkness had got the best of us.

I stood dead still for a moment, listening to something I'd never heard before and would never hear again. Nothing I had done that night had made any difference or would make any difference, and I took my hand away from the door and slipped back into my room across the hall. I slowly closed the door behind me and lay on the bed, listening to the ocean. I knew if I looked outside I would see that street light on the sandy pavement, and then I'd be crying, too. I lay there in the glow from the window and tried not to think about everything, and thought of nothing else.

Chapter 15

GAME OF PRICKS

Was I ever good at anything outside of work? There must have been something.

Basketball.

Basketball. That makes sense. How good was I?

You were more of a hustler than a technique man.

Did you ever see me play?

Oh yeah. Firsthand. Brutal.

I like it. Tell me everything.

To truly know my father, you had to play basketball against him. Basketball was the purest expression of Mike Nolan in physical form, and "physical" was the best word for it.

You read a lot about players who beat you mentally and physically. I hear sportswriters say it all the time, but for Mike, this was a very literal thing. He beat you with taunts and name-calling and questions about when you would be trying out for the girls' team this year. He beat you with elbows and pulled jerseys and hip-checks and occasionally a straight-up shove out of the way.

The man was a menace.

There was no such thing as being a kid on his court. I'd have a couple of friends over, and he'd saunter out of the garage with a ball under his arm and ask if we'd want to play. My friends, being kids, would say yes. What inevitably followed was a three-on-one massacre.

My old man would drain jump shots from three-point land and stuff any nine-year-old daring to venture into the paint.

A constant stream of abuse flew towards us while we were being pummeled all over the court, our shots rejected, our passes knocked out onto the lawn, and the score rapidly climbing to twenty-one to zip.

"Looking for your jock? Try looking in my pocket, pal."

"Come on, do something. What're you gonna do? Come on, Nancy."

"You're terrible. Do you know the rules? Any of them?"

He did not do this because he was mean. He did this because in his own twisted way he was trying to show you what he understood life to be: unfair, brutal, mocking, a vicious elbow if you invaded the wrong turf. His game was his life.

Basketball saved my old man, in a very real way. He was not a great student to begin with, and to make matters worse, he and Joe never saw eye to eye on his education. Mike wanted to go to school with all of his friends at St. Benedict's in Newark, but his mother Jeanne was having none of that. She wanted to fit in with the swank set around town, and they sent their kids up to Montclair Academy. Even the name conjures up visions of khaki-wearing country club larvae, and that's exactly what Mike found there. He hated the kids, he hated the teachers, he hated just about everything except the gym.

In between doing his best to fail out of as many classes as possible and dating my mother, all he did was play ball. He spent all of his time in that place, shooting baskets, as late as the staff would let him stay. They elected him captain as a sophomore, and he kept the job until he graduated.

Mike grew up playing on the old courts at Our Lady of the Lake in Verona, New Jersey. There he met one of his best friends, Bobby McCloskey, and the two of them were inseparable, until it came time to go to college. As lousy as Mike's grades were, they had not been bad enough to fail out of Montclair, make his old man see the light, and move him into Benedict's. They were almost bad enough that no college would want him and the Army would be the only route for him.

As it turned out, because Mike played ball, a small college called St. Vincent's out in Latrobe, Pennsylvania was interested, and so he went. Bobby didn't get to go to college, so Bobby became a Marine and went to Vietnam, and a sniper shot him dead in 1968.

Bobby drifted into one of the Subjects Never To Be Mentioned With Mike. I never once heard his name spoken by my father. Anything I heard came from my mother. She was the one to call him at college and tell him about Bobby. He didn't say anything; he just hung up the phone and showed up at her house the next day.

Mike carried a ball with him to the graveyard. He just silently stared at his friend's coffin, and then, after the burial, went to the old courts in Verona and took jump shots by himself for hours until Mom went and made him come home, way past dark. Some nights after that, she woke up to him whispering to himself in his sleep. He was saying "Bobby" over and over. After that night, he never mentioned Bobby again.

Mike gave me two books during my childhood, and Bob Cousy's *Basketball Is My Life* was one of them. I was eight years old, and it was Christmas. The book was not new; it was the old man's copy from when he was a kid. It sat under the tree amongst all the toys I'd received from my mother, each one more elaborately wrapped than the next, bearing the mark of her devotion to detail. Then there was a bunchy, Scotch-tape laden ball of paper in which Mike had wrapped up his old Cousy book.

I grabbed it first. The old man was not prone to wild displays of affection, and many is the man who worked for him who wondered if he had ever noticed his presence in all the years they'd shared the same office. Moving to a corner of the living room, away from my squealing, vapid, giggling little sisters, I ripped through the tape and paper and uncovered a green and yellow hardcover book with a black-and-white picture of some old-time basketball player wearing too-short shorts and Chuck Taylors. His face was intense and focused. It was the face of a man doing the thing he was made to do, and I liked that, he knew something I didn't. The paper cover was torn in places, and it had that old book smell to it.

The old man was standing over me, looking down on me and the book.

"Read that. It's all there." And he went back to taking pictures. I opened the book. On the first blank page, in black ink, appeared "Michael Nolan" in blocky, childish handwriting. Underneath that was fresh ink. "Read this. It's all here."

I read the book in the next few days, and here is what I remember, twenty-five years later. Cousy's parents were French immigrants in New York, maybe Brooklyn. Life was tough, and on top of everything else, Cousy was a lousy ballplayer. He broke his right hand at some point, so he learned to shoot with his left. I think he was sick a lot, and the other kids were nasty to him because he talked funny or maybe because his parents did. But he played and played and played. The kid shot the ball all the time, and he worked at this one thing, at basketball. He worked harder at it than seemed sane, his focus was amazing and he decided that, improbable as it seemed, this was his calling. He became a great player and went to the pros and won a bunch of titles with the Boston Celtics. At no point did you ever doubt that basketball was this man's life.

Mike never went to the pros. His knee gave out, his back gave out. Still he played on, nights at the YMCA in pickup games with guys from his office, against guys he barely knew. He would take me to his games and sit me in the bleachers with a Coke and tell me to watch. In the beginning, I did not know why I was there, or why of all books, he had given me Cousy's.

Mike's life had a rhythm and a pulse to it. On the court he knocked guys around, he dove after the ball, he yelled for it, he threw passes that had to be caught two-handed, like your coach always said they did. He shouted at you where to be, he let you know you were dogging it, he talked trash and asked you to do something about it. It was repulsive, and you couldn't stop watching, his voice boomed off the rafters and his body flew around the court. He worked sixteen-hour days, and weekends, and holidays and sometimes even Christmas, and at the office you could hear him booming down the hallways, and most times bodies flew then, too. And still he came out to the courts when he could.

One night there was an argument on the court. Someone, as someone was bound to, had had enough of Mike's shit. People were always having enough of his shit, and that was easily done, because he dispensed so much of it. I looked up from my can of Coke and there was yelling, the guy was saying he was tired, what the hell, it was a goddamn pickup game, just relax, and get a life, man. Mike was having none of it. He was disgusted—show up or don't show up, but come to play. It was the end of the game, anyway. People were going home, and he walked off the court alone.

He was still pissed off when we got in the car, so I said nothing. He sat there seething and fogging up the windows of the crappy old Toyota we'd bought used from the neighbors. On Bloomfield Avenue, we hit a red light. I could see him staring out the window at the cars rushing by, his head still out on the court somewhere. His hands dropped from the wheel. "People don't see how easy it is. They don't connect it in their heads, but it's so simple. All you have to do is decide that everything means everything. And then you'll never stop, because there's nothing else."

I didn't say anything, but after that, I knew why I was there on those nights at the Y, I knew why he gave me the book. Basketball was not my life. Nothing was yet my life. But I could learn.

I didn't have many friends, and I was no good at the game. Nobody really liked Mike, you could see that on the court, but they respected him, because he played like a killer out there. He had found his life in the game, and even though it turned out not to be his job, he worked his job like he worked an opponent. You could see how they grabbed his hand before the game started, with respect for the man. He was ferocious. He wanted me to find that, to get some game, to find my everything.

Chapter 16

DON'T TELL A SOUL

You know when I tell you that I barely remember anything after the
   accident that I'm not hiding anything from you or Kathy or the
   family. I just barely remember. I know it's better that I don't
   remember, for me. But it's not fair, I think that's the word I mean.
   It's not fair that happened to everyone else and not to me.

It came in bits and pieces, man. First you were dying. Then you
   weren't. Your friends came, my friends came, I remember all of
   that.

I should be lucky they came. I never really worked on them.

You did, in your own way. The ones that mattered, they showed.

OK.

The thing that is always the most important thing to remember about
   all the time you were gone is how much Kathy gave a shit about
   you, even after how bad you got with work and your own life in
   the end. You guys went so far back, nothing could shake her
   loose.

Who was this man? None of us had ever truly known. Now we would
never know. The August when the accident occurred slipped away
from us, and soon September was almost gone, too. The accident became The Accident. It dominated every facet of our family life now,
every conversation at the bar, every phone call from a friend, every
moment of meeting. It was the first thing anyone asked about and the
last thing they wished you well about.

In the weeks after, they barely woke Mike up. When I looked at
him lying there, the nerd in me could not help but think of Han Solo,

encased in carbonite, lying there helpless, hanging on Jabba's wall. We would talk to him, tell him who was in the room, tell him what we were up to. If he was "awake," his eyes would sometimes fall on you. Most of the time, he lay there sleeping, with tubes and wires hanging out of him. People would come in, change some tubes and change some wires, and then they would be off.

They were honest about the possibilities from the beginning. Nobody led us to believe there would be much to take home with us when it was all over. I pictured nurses living in my parents' house to take care of him, him not being able to feed himself, a perpetual look of dumb amazement on his face while he waited on death in a corner. Every day we went to visit him in the hospital was another day closer to that kind of outcome in my mind. I was certain with each passing day that more of his brain would be dying, and there would be less of him on the other end.

I would stand over him and look down at his head, wondering what was happening in there. If what was in there wasn't Michael anymore, he was dead. It was hard to tell. He was alive, but barely. The only sign of life was the almost imperceptible movement of his chest and the faint beeping of machines. A week after he had been hit, they mentioned it almost as an afterthought: all things staying equal, he lives. Beyond that, it's up to the patient.

Mike maintained an air of perpetual mystery every day of his life. People who had known him forever would not recall that he even owned a bike. His life was beyond compartmentalized, it was silent, hidden under layers of time and "conversations about other things," the way he used to describe having to talk to people about stuff he would rather not. His connection to the world around him was one long conversation about other things. If he did not want you to know, you never knew.

It got so that every lesson he had given you, every conversation you had ever had with him, you wondered whether any of it was real, whether he had really told you anything about himself or yourself, or whether he was just telling you what he wanted you to think about him. He was more about what he would never talk about than what he would.

At Christmastime, when I was very young, we would drive into the city, to the Diamond District. He would buy my mother one big present every year, and it was always made of diamonds. He had a special store run by two Jewish guys, and who knows how he had ever met them. We went to the same place every year, in vintage Mike Nolan fashion. A chorus of "Mr. Nolan!" and we would be swept into the back to view candidates for "Kathy's Big Gift" that year. I had no concept that this represented a big savings for the old man on a young prosecutor's salary at the time, or how important this was to him to be able to show Kathy that he was gradually making it in the world. I didn't know about things like that yet.

Mike and I would narrow down the selection to two or three items, and then we would go back and forth about the relative benefits of each of them. She'll like any of them, he said. She never had anything nice when she was a kid. So pick one.

One year I picked a ring she still wears today. It looks like two waves at the beach, crashing into one another. It was an inspired choice, and the old man loved it. On the way back to the car, I would hear something from him I'd heard often before. He would stress the importance of keeping a secret, of not telling a soul, not my mother, certainly, but not my sisters, or my friends, or any aunts or any uncles. Secrets have a way of leaking out if you weren't careful. If one person hears, it's as if everyone had heard.

"There's a secret to keeping secrets," he said, as we climbed into the car. "Never tell anyone anything." You could put it on his headstone. It was true. I never knew very much about him, and even though he was always talking, he never really said much. It was as if he was saying, you do not have to like me, but you can trust me, you can tell me anything, and it never goes any further. His discipline was inspiring that way. He wanted to be something, and every day when he woke up and saw the mold he had built for himself, he dove right into it. You never wanted to let him down, so I never once let any of our Christmas secrets out. I never told a soul; I didn't even tell them that I had a secret worth telling.

Kathy was never any the wiser. I would come down Christmas morning and see the ring on her finger, see her smiling and pointing it out to us, and I'd catch Mike's eye, and maybe behind her back he would give me a nod or a thumbs up. Even after Christmas had come and gone, I would never tell her I had known. There would be next year, and a new secret to keep.

They had been together since they were teenagers, and we gagged throughout our childhood at her stories about them. They had met in the church youth group, of which he was the leader, and it doesn't get any cornier than that. Until you asked Kathy if he was really into God, and she said probably not, he just liked being in charge of everything. He had to go to Montclair Academy, so he was captain of the basketball team. He had to go to church, so he was leader of the youth group.

I was fascinated by these stories, because none of us could ever imagine him as young, as a kid, as someone other than The Man In Charge Of The Situation Here. When I was ten, these stories made no sense. As I got older and spent my own time in high school and college, when she had known him growing up, they got a hell of a lot more interesting.

He used to call her four or five times a night, but he was calling just to talk; he didn't have the balls to ask her out. Imagine Mike Nolan, not having the balls. Unthinkable. She would talk with her sister, wondering when he was going to finally get around to it, or was he just not that interested in her. It got so that his calls were tying up the phone and pissing off Tom Murray, Kathy's old man, so much so that when he called, he would throw the phone down on the receiver and bellow at the top of his lungs, "Well, it was THAT MIKE NOLAN." And so, before he had ever even taken her out once, he had a nickname around the house: "That Mike Nolan." They disliked him before they ever even saw him.

Finally, he did work up the stones to ask her out, and their first date, because he was Mike Nolan and because he just had to hit a home run, was a Beach Boys concert. He showed up to her house on a motorcycle, which her mom took one look at and yelled at him from the front steps: "No daughter of mine is going anywhere on a motorcycle." So he came back with a convertible. What an asshole. They let her go anyway.

She didn't know his old man had cash. When he brought her home to meet his parents for the first time, she got one look at the house and started slapping his arm, telling him to quit kidding around and pull out of the driveway before these people called the cops. He laughed it off. It wasn't something he'd ever really had to think about.

They were inseparable. He only had eyes for her from that first date until the day they got married, eight years later. He kept his head down, working away at basketball and school until he hit the prosecutor's office. When she went to college, it almost all fell apart. She met someone else, and she told him. Mike was devastated, but he stopped calling, because the man had his dignity. I tried to think of him, back then, what he must have looked like when he lost something really big. I never saw him like that. It may have been the last time it ever happened before his last bike ride.

He had decided long before she dumped him that he was going to marry her, and you could picture him in law school, waiting on her, biding his time, keeping his focus and getting on with it. Kathy told me once about how they got back together. He had confronted her boyfriend, some guy named Harry, who was also in law school. She was really into Harry; she thought this was the guy for her. She was short about what happened after Mike visited or what had been said, but the results told the story: Harry tried to kill himself, and she ended up with Michael.

His relentlessness must have scared the shit out of the guy, like showing up to a fight after school behind the corner pharmacy and discovering that the other kid had fished one of Daddy's guns out of the closet. What he had thought would be a typical confrontation had suddenly turned into a lesson in How Things Really Are, and maybe the guy wasn't really up to it, seeing what might be out there for him. He became a professor and stayed out of the courtroom, and that encounter with the old man probably made it an easy decision for him.

He asked her on the beach, in the town we would grow up in. It was in late March, and by the time she got back to her house, it was April 1st and nobody believed her. The kid who nearly failed out of high school? That kid? THAT MIKE NOLAN? You're gonna marry that jerk? Her kid sister laughed in her face and told her she got the ring in a bubblegum machine at the mall.

No one was laughing a month later when they had to have the Nolans over for an engagement party. This was the Murrays' first daughter, and they were not fancy people, but they'd stocked up on champagne and orange juice for mimosas. They were not counting on a dozen Nolans descending on the joint, demanding Scotch when it was barely even noon and rummaging through the refrigerator when they didn't like what had been set out. They did not care for the belching, or the backslapping, or the consumption of every single bit of alcohol they could lay their hands on. Or the declarations in the middle of the afternoon that they were leaving and heading into Newark to go to McGovern's, because at least that joint probably wouldn't run out of booze. No, no one was laughing, but Mike and Kathy were getting married, and everyone could just get used to it.

They did. And nine months and three weeks later, I came along. It was said the families were down in the waiting room while I was born, trying to work out the math. Welcome to your world, junior.

He only let a few people see the good in him.

The problem was that hardly anybody else knew that he actually did care about the whales. His whales were the kids in Newark he had seen on his visits back to the city where he was born. He had seen their poverty, their lack of education, their disease, and contrasting it with the money and opportunity he saw around himself, decided that it wasn't fair. He saw the towering impossibility of really changing any of it, but he was an unreasonable man, and had taken G.B. Shaw's advice to heart. All progress would depend on people like him. He started a little organization called Kids Corporation that educated these kids and gave them something to eat. It started out as a few kids teaching after school and by the time of his accident, thousands of them were in his programs.

Everyone knew about Kids Corporation. They knew he hustled

time and cash for kids from Newark, even if most of them really never knew why. Most people never asked. They saw him don a Santa hat at Christmastime and go around his law office with a sack demanding presents for the kids in Newark, this guy who could seem like the antithesis of that particular day. I had asked him about it once, and like most of his answers, it was brutally simple. "We got to leave Newark and have it good, they had to stay and have it bad. This is the deal. Nothing's for free."

When you cultivate the image of being an asshole, though, people are more than willing to buy into it. With Mike, people just made the assumption and never got much further than that.

Nobody knew the real him. Not even us. He did the right thing by strangers and friends alike anonymously, and mostly for people he'd just heard about who needed something. When I was a kid, he and I would load the car up after Mass on Christmas Eve and drive to the houses of people he knew with big families and small paychecks. We'd leave presents on porches and in driveways, and pull away. He never talked when we delivered; even that was like a job to him, the same way he'd get up in the morning and go to work. It was just how it was done.

In college, I had acquaintances who got letters from the priest in their dorm, telling them an anonymous benefactor would pay for their books for the semester, or maybe give them some money for tuition. It was only after the third or fourth time that I figured it out; he was picking people he'd met at football games or weekends when he was teaching at the law school. I'd have told him something about somebody, and he had a friend in the administration he'd work through. I heard it all from Kathy, but not until I called and asked.

His dad had done the same when he was in college. It was just a thing for him, too. If you asked him about it, he'd clam right up. That kind of thing was never discussed.

"Keep it like a secret," he'd say. "Don't tell a soul."

All this from a guy who loved telling you how he didn't really like other people very much.

If you had asked me what I wanted for my family before The Accident, I would have had the same answer for decades: to be normal people. I thought that someday, Mike and I would sit down, like regular guys, like I imagined my friends and their dads, and we would talk. I would tell him how I had felt about him when I was a kid, the strange mix of awe and fear he inspired in me, how if it had not been for him, I would never have had half the opportunities or a quarter of the drive I have now. That even today, at work and close to forty, there is a part of me that wonders what he would say about my day's little successes and failures, whether he would have cared. And that every night I stayed late, every weekend I worked, it was his foot still on the pedal somewhere in my head. We would sit and talk, maybe out on the deck at the beach, about things I had always wanted for him and for me, and we would move on. We would just be two regular guys.

But more than anything, I always wanted to tell him I went back to his father's house for him on the last night they ever spoke. I wanted to tell him that I had tried for him, gone to bat for him when it had really counted, that I was loyal and unafraid, like he always was. How Joe was my best friend, how well he had always treated me, how much I had liked him better than Mike, and how quickly I had walked away from him when he threw in against my father. Sometimes you wait a little too long to get it out there, so long that if you did, they wouldn't matter any more. They surely wouldn't now.

I thought of what I knew about him, and would never know about him, sitting there in his room, staring at him. All of the questions I had now, that had never occurred to me in all the years that I knew him, because after all he was there, and either we would be like that one day, or we never would. Either way, he would just be there.

I know nothing about you. All I know, someone else told me. And I'd always meant to ask.

When it came down from the doctors, it came down quick.
They woke him up a few weeks after the accident, slowly taking

him off of the drugs that had kept him in a coma. Calls went out to friends to say that today was the day, it was all coming soon, he would come back. There was no dramatic wake-up, it came in pieces, a fluttering of the eyes here, and slight move of the hand there. We just watched him, four people and some visitors, waiting on the man.

He would sometimes flail his arms around, and when his eyes were open, you'd sit with him and say anything you could think of. Talk to him, the doctors said. He knows you're there. Kathy talked to him every second she could, about all the usual things, about her days, as if she didn't spend every day sitting in the hospital with him. About what we kids were all doing, as if we weren't all sitting around thinking of him. About all the friends who came to see him.

In truth, very few people outside of the immediate family were allowed anywhere near him. No one from his firm was allowed in. No one from the family he no longer spoke to. No old friends, not my friends, no one. Only people Mike and Kathy had known since they were kids, that was it. She took care of him that way, she knew he would never have allowed anyone to see him like this, all torn up and broken down. She and I would confer about any visitors: yes they can, no they wait.

She would stroke his hair and tell him how soon he would be out, how fast he would be going home, if he was good, if he took it easy and thought about getting better.

His old friends, Joe and Anthony came. I watched them watching him, wondering what it must be like to see your guy knocked out like that. They knew him so much better than I did. They had lived with him on cases for months and years, spent weekends in conference rooms and hotels and out on the road. They were like a legal rock band, and their head songwriter was in rehab, and now what the fuck do we do? These guys were cool as Christmas, walking in almost every day, going miles out of their way every morning, these important guys, greeting him with a "Hey, pal," and then going about their day. They barely said anything else, and when they needed to, these two best friends of his, they would look over at me, and the three of us would walk out of the room. They liked Kathy, but these were old-school guys, they talked to the son. That was that.

It was always a nod to Kathy, "She need anything?"

No.

"You need anything?"

No.

"Call if anything happens, guy." A few slaps on the back, and they were gone. In those little moments in the hallway, I made it a point to be better to my friends, to be there like that, night and day if I had to. Guys like that make the difference.

It was on one of those mornings that I first heard him speak. For weeks he had been silent. I could see him from outside his room, Kathy sitting talking to him, and occasionally he looked like he was moving his lips, like he was talking back to her. We were told this was next to impossible. It was highly unlikely that he had the ability to speak, between the brain injury and the damage to his throat from the tubes, but still you could see him trying. The ear, nose and throat doctors would come in and talk about how difficult a road he had, and the old man would sort of stare at them along with us, and then, as the doctor left, he would go on trying to whisper to Kathy.

Mike's friend Joe had come in one morning, and Kathy was talking to him. "Look, Mike, Joe's here."

"Hey, pal." That was it for a while. Joe and I talked in the corner about insurance and money and arrangements that needed to be made.

"OK," I said. "See you tomorrow."

"OK, man," he said to me.

"See ya, pal," he said to Michael.

"Bye-bye, Joe," said Michael. We all looked around the room, like the metal shelves had just started waving at us. No one had heard his voice in months. It may have been decades since Joe had been surprised by anything, and he seemed to have lost his words. "Bye-bye, Mike," he finally said.

I walked him out. "Well," I said. "Did you get what you came for?"

"Sure did, pal. That's what it's all about, right there, man."

"We should tell the doctors."

"Tell them? Tell them what? They don't tell you anything. Keep that one. Keep it like a secret."

Chapter 17

GET ME AWAY FROM HERE, I'M DYING

When can I go home? And where is it? That's what you'd ask me all the
   time.

Who can blame me? Home is pretty great.

You didn't know that.

I didn't know anything.

Framed by the hospital's window, Mike stood looking out on a street
full of kids. I would stand in his doorway on those days and nights
when I could make it out of the city, in my suit and tie, looking like he
used to look when he came home from work. He had picked out this
suit for me, blue with pinstripes, a white shirt and a blue tie. I would
find him like this almost every time, standing by himself, looking
out the window at the kids in the street, at the crappy neighborhood
around the rehab hospital, figuring it all out, trying to figure out how
he had arrived here.

They moved him to the best rehab clinic on the East Coast from
the hospital at the beach after a few months. It was a twenty-minute
drive from my apartment. In the hospital, they had one job: save his
life and preserve as much of the rest of him as they possibly could.
They'd done that. Mike was alive, and he looked the same way he did
the day before the truck hit him.

Now he was in the place where they would save what was left in that rock hard head of his. The Kessler Rehabilitation Center. If you were here, things were bad.

When something happens to you out of the blue that divides your life into Before and After, you either refer to it as the lodestone that changed everything, or you never talk about it at all. In time, the only thing we ever talked about became "The Accident." It was referred to in the same alternating tone of disgust and dread with which people referred to "The War." "The Accident" drew a line under one life and started something entirely different. Now, you look back and it all seems like one clean break: today life is one thing, before, it was something else. Things don't really happen that way. They build on one another, a woeful addition of trial and quiet pleading.

Waking up each day, you were sure this was not happening, because this is not how it was supposed to go, there was no room for this in The Big Plan. This was the kind of thing that happened to other people, and those people hired people like Mike to clean up the mess. When you're Winston Wolf, you never expect to be the body in the backseat.

Mike didn't like surprises. Wherever we went, he liked to know the place, he liked to know the people, and he wanted everything to be the same as the last time. He loved to walk into a restaurant or a shop and have everyone know him. He liked the staff to know what he liked, to call him "Mr. Nolan" and to wave them off magnanimously and say, "Please, call me Michael," which of course meant, "Call me Mr. Nolan."

Weeks could go by without a word between us, not because of any particular feud, but because we were busy. And if I wasn't busy, I wanted him to think I was busy. Being busy was his thing, and to call him was to advertise to him that it was not your thing. You were admitting you had time on your hands for idle talk. He would always take my call, he just would not like it.

If you ever heard from him, it would be a call from a secretary, from a blocked number.

"Hello?"

"Sean. It's your father's office."

"Hi."

"Your father wants to know if you're available tomorrow night in New York."

"Go figure, he lives in New York. What for?"

"He didn't say. So?"

"Sure."

I would show up at the office with its big comfortable chairs and total lack of decent reading material and wait for him. He was always on time for me; he never kept me waiting. It was as if it would be disloyal to leave his kid sitting out there where everyone else could see him.

The wooden double doors would burst open, and he'd be standing there, smiling, maybe nodding his head a little, as if to say, "Hey, huh. Check this place out, right? How great is this?"

He'd have his briefcase in hand, and I'd have to be already moving with him as he strode through the lobby or else he'd be waiting in the elevators by the time I got there.

"What are we up to?"

"They didn't tell you?"

"No, did you tell her?"

"I never tell her anything. They already know too much."

The taxi dropped us off at one of the places Mike liked. The old man would refer to these establishments as "classy places," as in, "Antonio's? Classy place." In the old school of Irish-America, "classy place" meant "foreign accent." Mike loved this kind of shop; give him someone with a Continental accent and chances are he would dub it a classy place if you asked him about it.

"Hey, hey, hey, Mr. Nolan."

"Roberto, how are you? When are you going to start calling me Mike?"

"Mr. Nolan, never. Your son is with you."

"That's him."

"Time for suits?"

"He looks like shit. You have to help him."

"He looks great. But we help anyway."

We would all smile, and then the hard part would start. Mike dressed well. He looked classic without trying. When you looked at him, you knew he was some big shit lawyer. I have never known what I like wearing, and I don't particularly like shopping. At all. The old man would pick out a few things and take them over to Bob for inspection, and I would have to try them on for the two of them.

Mike and the suit guy looked at me with their noses up in the air.

"Stand up."

"Throw your shoulders back."

"Put your glasses on.'

"Nah, take them off."

"What do you think, Bob?"

Roberto would shrug. "Really? He looks like a salesman."

"He is a fucking salesman. He's a salesman for the bank."

"OK, OK," I said. "I'll take the suit. For the love of God."

Mike was a ghost. That was the only way I could wrap my head around the person standing in front of me, staring out the hospital window. His body was the same, but it wasn't him anymore. His shoulders slumped, his head hung down, he walked slowly, one foot dragging ever so slightly across the floor.

In a sick way, the rehab hospital was encouraging, because Mike was easily the least fucked up person in treatment. A lot of patients made you wonder how they had survived their initial injuries. They were missing big pieces of their bodies, and most of them were semi-catatonic, staring into space and drooling. I avoided them, and felt no shame in doing so. No one could say how close my old man had come to being like them, and whether he ever knew my name or spoke another word again, the guy would be something, we knew that much by then.

They took him up from the beach by ambulance with my mother sitting next to him, I was at work when she texted me, "Thunder Road has brought him a bit closer to home today." I folded up my phone, walked into the hallway and held my head against the wall. I wanted to bang it again and again until my forehead bled. He owned that road in his old car, flying down to the beach at unheard of speeds, not giving a shit, blaring the radio, knowing every bend in the road so well that he could close his eyes and drive it. Now he rode helplessly up to one more stop on the Long Decline.

I took great pride in never once having ever given my real name when signing in to the hospital. Mike Nolan had a steady stream of regular visitors, from Bartholomew Bigballs to Kilgore Trout to John Galt to Filthy McNasty. He drew a popular and dangerous crowd, and I think he would have wanted it that way.

I would hang back, watching him from behind everyone else. People talked to him a lot, asking him things, but all he did was stare at the walls, occasionally nodding or shaking his head. He had a big room, and we hung things on the walls to remind him of his old life: letters from people he knew, posters of Notre Dame, pictures he liked, stickers and drawings from the children Kids Corporation had helped. I printed out the lyrics to Townes Van Zandt's "To Live Is To Fly" and stuck them up, but no one else seemed to like the song, and maybe they were more for me than for him.

Every day, the doctors came to talk to my mother. They'd speak about Mike while he was him sitting in front of them, as if he wasn't there. I wanted to tap them on their shoulders and whisper, "He's right here, you know. He can hear you. Show some respect." They didn't, though. They spoke to us from the corner of the room, and we listened to them read from the Book of Revealed Medicine and nodded along.

The truth is, they tell you nothing. I never understood whether it was because they didn't know or because they wanted to play down expectations. Maybe they thought a lawyer like him would sue them if they said he'd get better and then didn't. We drifted through weeks of ballpark estimates.

Will he get better? Maybe, they'd say. Every patient is different.

It depends on where they start from and how much they actually want to get better.

I listened to them, picking up their throwaway sentences and holding on to fragments of hope. I scanned Mike's face for anything that reminded me of the old him. In the beginning it was hard, because he had no words, and that was the most radical change. He had been highly a verbal man: profane, sarcastic and hilarious. The man in the Notre Dame sweatshirt, staring up at the ceiling and saying nothing, was none of those things. I didn't know him.

"Nobody feels sorry for us."

"Nobody should."

"No. Nobody should."

Mom and I were in the house, getting clothes for Mike to wear in the hospital: track suits and socks and loose fitting T-shirts. She had repeated one of the old man's stock phrases, an old joke between his father and him. They would say it while reflecting on their luck. Although they worked their asses off, they barely claimed any credit for their good fortune, always quick to say how lucky they were.

I tried not to feel sorry for us. In hospitals, you meet people worse off than you, people with terrible injuries, with no money, no insurance and no bail-out from anyone. I felt sorry for them and hoped they didn't feel sorry for me.

Mostly, there was just so much silence. When someone asks me what it was like after his accident, that's the word I use. Silence. It was a long quiet that might never have ended. Before, there was a perpetual roar and shouting and noise. In its place lay a body that didn't move and a head that didn't talk. Strangers came in and took care of a man who spent his life protecting and persecuting other strangers, now a guy who could barely dress himself anymore.

When there is no hope in a situation, when no one can throw you a line, you create your own. This wasn't for me. I could have accepted it if Mike were gone forever. I would have hated it, but he had made me into the kind of person who could move along without him. The same was not true for my mother. This would be hers to deal with, her problem to solve, her life to rebuild. My life had no real structure and no one depended on me. My only routine was work and weekends with my friends, a steady rhythm that I had successfully maintained for years. There was no other side of the coin for me, this was it. For her, the land on the other side of the bridge had floated away.

I said to her, "You know he's coming back to us. One way or the other. We'll get him back."

"I know."

"We can make this good. He's broken every record so far. He's kicked ass. Everything the doctors have said that he probably wouldn't be able to do, he did. The man is a machine."

"I know what you're doing. I appreciate it. Let's just see how it goes and keep expecting nothing.'"

She walked out to the car with a few gymbags full of clothes. I stood there in Mike's closet, looking through all of his suits, remembering the ones we'd picked out together, and a few that we owned in common. My suits were drab black, and always I wore blue ties. There really wasn't much to them. His were like armor. Shiny and black, like knives in a dark kitchen, they meant business.

I looked past the suits and saw racks and racks of ties, all kinds of colors, all kinds of crazy designs I would never have had the balls to buy. He knew my reluctance, and yet he'd never bought me a tie. "Well, you son of a bitch, you won't be needing these anytime soon." I grabbed handfuls and shoved them in my bag. Every situation had its minor benefits and now, like the bastard I was, I scurried out of the house. It was what the old man would have wanted.

After a few months, the conversation stopped being just one way. He found his voice again, but it was different. He could barely talk, maybe a few words a day.

Better days were coming, I would say that to anyone who asked.

How's he doing? Better days are coming. What's with your old man? Better days are coming. I told anyone who would listen, his colleagues, his friends, my friends, even his doctors. This train is bound for glory, I'd say. Things go off the track sometimes, they're coming back. You think a prick like this just folds it up and goes home because of something like this? They would have had to kill him for that to happen. But they didn't. They missed, so to hell with them.

Mostly, I said it to him.

He did not know who I was in the hospital. When he arrived, it was pretty clear he didn't know who anyone was or what had happened to him. We spoke to him about what was going on outside the hospital walls as if he could follow. We told him that my sister Michaela had taken over the running of Kids Corporation for him, that his friends and his firm were taking care of everything, that there was nothing for him to worry about other than getting home.

Mike's attraction to Kathy was immediate. His mind was destroyed, but it wasn't like some dog that follows you around just because you feed it. It was like watching gravity take hold of a foreign object, the way he straightened when she walked into the room, how he would pull his sweatshirt down and try to look at her, throw his shoulders back, look like a man. He may not have been able to articulate who she was anymore, but she was someone to him, more than anyone else, right from the start. He remembered her name first, weeks before he knew anyone else.

In the early days you would fight for every little moment you could get that showed you that there was still some of him left in that shell. We snuck beers into his room on a Saturday in October to watch the Notre Dame game. Sitting by his bedside, we tried to make it feel like everything was normal, the five of us sitting around, drinking beer, watching the Irish. We talked to him about the significance of the game, why this team mattered, how much he loved the place, but there was no recognition from him. He stared off into space, looking at the TV only intermittently. Every new beer made it seem a little less like home, until the team took the field. They came running out of the tunnel, and Mike lifted up his arm and made a fist. I put my hand out, and he high-fived me. I got through a lot of nights on that.

Weeks wore on, and he kept getting better. Each time I came, I brought an index card with one of his typical sayings on it. I'd hand it to him and make him say the line over and over again. When we finished the drill, I'd tack the card on his board. When he looked up at it, he could see his greatest hits, all lined up on the wall.

"Hey Mike. Got your new phrase. You ready?"

He took that extra moment to focus on me, to know who I was. "Hey, Sean."

"How've you been?"

"OK, I guess." He wore a look of almost permanent surprise now, which should have shocked no one, since everything happening every day was going to be a big surprise from now on.

"Come on aboard for the Big Win."

Before every sentence he spoke, there were at least three or four seconds of dead air, while he collected himself. "What's that mean?"

"It's you, pal. It's something you always said. Come on aboard for the Big Win."

"What's the Big Win?"

"The Big Win is whatever mission you're on today. Right now the Big Win is to get you the hell out of this place."

"I hate it here. I just want to go home."

"I know you do, man. The more you talk and the more you can remember, the sooner they're going to let you go."

"I mean, this must be what jail is like."

"It's a pretty swank jail, though."

"Come on aboard for the Big Win. OK. I'm on board."

"Good. Stick around for the happy ending."

He laughed and paused. "Was that another one of mine?"

"Sure was. It's right here on the board from last week."

He shuffled over and touched the different things people had hung up for him. He spoke very slowly. "This is all me? This is all the stuff I used to say, and all the stuff I used to like? All here?"

"It's all you, Mike. This is how you come back, guy. Piece by piece. All the little things like this, they add up, they made you Mike, and if you learn them all, you'll be you all over again. That's how it works."

"OK. Thanks."

"Thanks for what? Wait 'til you get the bill."

"Is that another one?"

"Hell yes."

We would walk up and down the hallways and into the exercise rooms. I'd meet his physical therapists and his nurses, shake their hands, ask if he was behaving himself while he smiled and looked embarrassed. He would walk beside me with his arm around my shoulders to lean on. This was a different thing for us now; I could not remember ever being closer than three feet away from him. Mike Nolan had always been a guy who radiated a very clear sense of Space That Was Mine and Space That Was Yours. Yours was whatever was not his. And yours was smaller.

The conversations were almost always the same. He wanted out. He'd heard about a beach house, and a job and an office in New York. Those sounded good. Let's get back to those.

Soon, Mike, I'd say. Weeks rolled past, and as his fog began to lift, he slowly began to show an ability to remember things from one day to the next, even if they were little fragments. He would ask after your job. He couldn't remember what it was, but he knew it was in New York. He'd ask after your girlfriend. He didn't know her name or what she looked like, but he knew there was one. Those were the good days, the days you got out to your car and felt that, even with everything else gone, if there were more days like that, you could do it. You could get home on days like that.

There were so many new things about him every time I came to visit. There were new questions, new wants, things that had never come up before. He would steal chocolate from anywhere he could get it. One day I came in to find him absentmindedly munching on a Ding Dong. This man would never have had anything to do with something as frivolous or ridiculous-sounding as a Ding Dong.

"Christ, is that a Ding Dong? They still make those?"

"Yeah," he said. He threw the box, still half full, in my direction. "It's a Ding Dong, all right. Don't eat too many. They're mine."

"Where'd you get these?"

"The guy across the hall."

I looked across the hall. The patient in question looked as he always did: completely comatose. The guy was brain dead or nearly so.

"Where'd you really get them?"

He shrugged his shoulders. "He gets visitors. They left them in there. So I stole them. Have you seen the guy? He ain't eating them."

I had never seen him go red in the face. The man never gave a shit about what people thought. Now he put his head down and sheepishly laughed whenever someone swore, or reacted like a gun had gone off if there was a noise far down the hallway. Or if you found him stealing food from the brain dead.

And still the old parts of him shone through the fog more clearly every day. I would test him, throw out the things that would have provoked the old him to say something back. They were the little things I would wrap up in my head when I left, walking to the parking lot, wondering how we had all gotten here.

"Well at least the girls who work here are all hot," I said.

"I tell you, pal. There's an upside to everything. Sometimes you can't fucking beat it."

"Too right, man." I stopped in the hallway, still feeling the faint echo of his words bouncing off of the tiles, and I was glad for that little sound of the real him, somewhere deep in his head, struggling to get out.

Kathy would get regular updates from the therapists, how his memory was improving and whether he was ready yet to go back to whatever pieces of his old life he would be able to carry forward with him. Every day he went to classes and worked, doing what looked like cardio to me, throwing balls while running, that kind of thing. They would assess his ability to assimilate to the world outside, their world back in New York. There were dexterity tests for his body and for his mind, frequent updates on his progess, and a constant leveling of our expectations.

When Kathy came in one day, they told her that he just was not ready yet. They had been giving him a variety of real-life tests to see how he would do, and he was failing most of them. He could not tell them how to get the subway, he did not know where to get a bottle of milk, he could not say how much a newspaper cost. She quietly explained to him that the man had not been in a store in almost twenty years. He had not bought milk or anything else in that long; there would just not have been any time in his day. And he walked to work every day, he never took the subway.

They laughed. How could someone function like that? Who ever heard of such a thing? What kind of life could this man have led?

You didn't know him, she said. He wasn't like other people. Before, this had been her excuse for his every indiscretion, his sneering at strangers, his fits, his swearing. You don't know him. Now three men in white coats sat in front of her, declaring how preposterous this concept was.

"He's going to have to be like other people, Kathy. He's going to have to live a normal life now."

She would smile and nod her head. What else could she do? They didn't understand how much of an exception he had always been.

Michaela was his most frequent visitor. She would leave her office in Newark at Kids Corporation and drive over to see him every day. She would show up at his door and go to lunch with him in the cafeteria. Michaela was a talker, she always had been. She didn't start until she was nearly two years old, but then she never shut up. When she was a kid, I would throw something at her every time she walked into a room, because if you gave her an opening, she would only start in with some stupid rambling about what she thought of clouds and where sheep came from and why her new bedspread had flowers on it. Around our house, if anyone mentioned a "Michaela story," you knew it was one without any beginning, middle or end—just one long line of babble.

And so, for his sins, Mike Nolan was visited by a champion blabbermouth on a daily basis. As much as he could talk now, I'm sure he barely got a word in. It took him a few seconds after any sentence someone said to process the information. You could see him staring over your shoulder while his brain digested every word and he formulated a response. It would get better with time, but here, in Kessler, he was still taking it all in very slowly.

His head must have been spinning as he watched this girl come in and talk him into the ground. She was so good, coming to see him every day, and I have no doubt she left feeling sadder than almost anyone else besides Kathy. Michaela had worked with him every day since she had graduated college, spending her time helping him fulfill a dream he'd had since he was a kid. Now, to see him helpless like this, instead of a strong leader, telling her and the rest of the staff what to do every day—that must have been tough.

Still, she had slipped effortlessly into his role at Kids Corporation, taking control of all of the things he had done, which amounted to raising cash and kicking ass. No doubt as she sat there, talking the old man's ear off, day in and day out, she felt a certain pride in what she had done, that she had kept his dream alive and well on the streets of Newark, that kids were still being educated and fed and going to their doctors.

And I knew she waited for the day he would walk back through the door and she could hand him back the keys and tell him that it was better than he'd left it.

One night he and I were talking in the hallways, doing our walk up and down the corridors, speaking conspiratorially about the nurses, which ones looked slow, which ones he could probably get by, which ones were the good-looking ones. He had been planning his escape for some time, thinking that if they didn't let him out, he'd pull an Andy Dufresne on them.

By now, you could believe that he was getting his head around at least some of what was going on. He was able to converse, and his memory seemed to be functioning, at least on a level that assured you that tomorrow he would recognize your face the next day and every day after that. You knew that he had made a mental Who's Who of important faces and people and could stick to it. You hoped for that much at least.

"Hey, man," he said. "I've got a question for you."

"OK. Is it about your therapists? Because I am eventually going to have to tell Kathy about this fixation."

"No, it's not that. Who is this annoying girl that shows up for lunch here every day? She just won't shut the hell up."

//

Chapter 18

IT MAKES NO DIFFERENCE

I still think about work all of the time. I wish I had something to do,
somewhere I had to be every day.

I know you do. You're here, though, and you have to be happy for
everything we have now.

You say "we" a lot.

There are no ordinary stories around guys like us. Nobody ever just
did something and was done with it. No one ever just served in the
Army. We served in the army, and we fought from the beaches to
Berlin, and we killed five hundred fucking Nazis with our bare hands.
Nobody ever just had a drinking problem. We made it an entire town's
problem, burning our own houses down and barfing in the street and
destroying the neighbors' property.

Things had to be extraordinary. There was no run-of-the-mill.
Whatever it was you did, or whatever it was you were about, there had
to be a story behind it all, something to tie it all together. It had to be a
part of The Big Story. Mike Nolan's Big Story was, of course, work.

The legend insisted that he was not that smart a guy. Many a work
story began, "Now, I was not the smartest guy in the room. That guy
was Biff Awesome, III. He didn't count on me, though. Anyway, . . ."
The story, according to those who told it, was that his success had
nothing to do with brains, but everything to do with the fact that
he worked his ass off. Apparently in every job he had ever had, even
though he was the least intelligent person there, he beat everyone else
by working them into the ground.

The allegory that tied it all together was the story of him and my mother on vacation when I was just a kid. He was an associate in a law firm, and he and another guy were working for one of the big deal partners. The other guy was on vacation at the same time, and a call went out to both of them that there was trouble with a case they had been working on, and the firm needed them to come back right away. Mike hopped the next flight from Bermuda. The other guy didn't. That was the lesson. This story would be recounted whenever you were deemed lazy or not sufficiently motivated to bust your ass doing whatever needed to be done.

Mike loved to talk about work, not just his own, but the stuff everyone else needed to be doing. There was always something to be done, and God help you if he caught you watching kung-fu movies on Channel 5 if the cars had not been washed or the lawn had not been mowed. The old man was like the Marines—he'd sooner watch you dig holes and fill them back up again than see you sitting around enjoying yourself.

He would come home on a Wednesday night and cheerfully begin talking about the weeding that needed to be done around the house, the washing of the cars, the trimming of the pathway, you name it. He could put you to work faster than a Siberian prison camp commandant. My sisters did so much damn weeding that they came to resemble those Vietnamese ladies you see crouching in rice paddies. They had the same forlorn, how-the-hell-do-I-get-out-of-here look on their faces, and their jobs were just as hopeless.

As we sat in the waiting room in the hospital near the beach, I imagined my mom and my sisters were wondering about whether he would live, whether he would be himself again, whether we would be ourselves again. I wondered whether he would work again. Without work, he would be utterly lost in the world. I could not imagine him without his job, and I doubt anyone else could either. It was how he was connected to nearly everything in his life, and without it, there were no friends, no lunches, no dinners, no parties, no phone calls, no e-mails. There would be no reason to get up in the morning or to come home at night. There would be one big nothing.

In rehab, he started to talk about work. In the beginning, he just wanted to go home, even when he didn't know where it was. He learned the words "New York." He wanted to be able to remember people, and so he learned "Joe" and "Kathy" and "Anthony." What he really wanted was his old life back, and it didn't take long for him to start remembering what that was all about.

He learned things by osmosis, by picking up what was said around him. Some days that amounted to nothing, some days it was more. It depended on whether there was something significant he could hang a piece of himself on, look at, and recognize a bit of himself in it. He asked questions, once, twice, a hundred times. Most of the time, there was nothing to grasp, but when there was, he grabbed a hold of the idea and held on with a death grip. One of them was the word "attorney."

I was not there on the day that he learned what he used to be, but one night when I came to see him, something fundamental had shifted within him.

I did my thing, peeking in the open door and knocking on the doorjam as if he had any choice about me coming in.

"Old man."

There was a five-second pause while he matched my name to my face.

"Sean."

"How're we doing?"

"I'm an attorney. I don't know if you know about that."

I didn't say anything for a bit. He looked proud of himself. Here was something at last that he owned, something concrete he could tell people: I am this thing.

"I know something about it. Where did you hear about being an attorney?"

"I don't know." He was smiling. "But someone better fill me in on it."

There was a chair next to his bed, and I put my jacket over its back and sat down.

"Jesus Christ, man."

His eyes glimmered. Somewhere behind them was that evil old bastard trying to get out. He put his hand on my shoulder.

"From what I hear, He's got nothing to do with it."

What does an attorney do when he can't remember the law? What does he do when he can't remember a single case he ever tried, or a single client, a single word he ever wrote or the minute of a meeting he'd sat in on? If he needed to start from dead zero, what would he do?

He would spend ten hours a day watching "Law & Order," that's what he'd do. One cannot appreciate how many times a day that show is on TV until you spend a few days with a severely brain-damaged lawyer trying to get his mojo back by watching the only show he can find that features courtroom action for ten solid hours a day across five different cable channels.

What began as a question from his hospital bed grew into an obsession as days filled with physical rehabilitation gave away to days at home with nothing to do but wonder what it was he used to do all day. How did you fill up all of this time? Everyone would tell you how much you used to bust your ass, but what did that mean? The days get long when there's nothing but staring out the window, wanting to get back to whatever it was you used to do that got you through every day. Mike couldn't remember his work, and no one could really describe it to him. What you could explain to him, he wasn't ready to understand yet.

He would attack the problem at the margins, and on my visits to see him in the apartment, it gradually became clear that he had developed an agenda, a mission.

Mom told me about the "Law & Order" issue, not long after they brought him home from rehab and he had discovered the wonder of 500 channels.

"We might need to get a second TV."

"Why?"

"He's watching 'Law & Order' all the time."

"He never watched TV before. Maybe it's good for him to finally be into something."

"I'm talking all day here. He watches that show all day."

"You don't think it's . . ."

"Oh yeah. It is. He thinks these are instructional videos or something."

So began his slow, steady mission to someday return to work. The legacy of work in his past must have etched some sort of pattern on an uninjured part of his brain, enough for him to see no fulfillment in a life devoid of something to do. I know a lot of men could have folded in circumstances like that, could have wrapped it up, taken the big insurance payout, and retired twenty years early. It didn't make him any better than them, it just made him Mike.

Now, sitting next to him on the couch watching TV, he would casually start up a conversation that was actually anything but casual. He would repeat the same questions sometimes, but with each asking, he was grasping for a bit more of the past.

"Was I on the phone a lot?"

"Did I use a computer?"

"I had clients. What were they like?"

"What kind of people did I work with?"

"Was I any good at all of this?"

The months went by. Mike saw his doctors and rehabilitation specialists every day. He carried a legal pad with him everywhere, and he bought himself a daily planner. At the front of it, in big block letters he had written, "GOAL #1: GET BACK TO WORK." No one could mistake the intent of his every waking moment.

The rehab people tried to get him to focus on short-term goals, like remembering faces and names and incidents that had occurred a few days before. He worked at developing the crutches people who have suffered severe damage use to get through their days. He wrote everything down. His notepads were full of reminders to himself: who he talked to, what time of day, where he'd been, things he told people.

The grim monotony belied the sadness these notes inspired in any-one who had known him before the accident, because they belonged to a man who had been totally in control of his world. As the weeks and months slipped by, the notepads didn't get smaller; they grew as he tried harder and harder to regain control over his memories and his life. What had been a half a page of random phone calls or visits to the doctor turned into a record of conversations he'd had, the times he'd had them, what they'd talked about, whether he'd promised anything or needed to remember something.

I'd see him sitting on the couch, poring over the books, as if the repetition of reading could somehow reinforce these every day experi-ences that kept slipping away from him.

Gradually, my hope for him began to slip away. In its place was not despondency, but rather a feeling like I was a fan of a perpetually losing sports team. I rooted for him in the same way, with the same "Come on, guys, you can do it" feeling even though I knew they prob-ably could not.

In March, the doctors laid it out for him. There were charts and explanations, a sober analysis of the effects of the impact on his brain, a thorough assessment of required mental processing speeds, of judg-ment and timing. Mike had to hear it from them, from the eggheads, so that he knew this was no bullshit; this was the new real.

When they were finished, he sat upright in his chair, in his suit and tie, as he had so many times in so many courtrooms. He regarded them with that poker face of his, while he thought about everything they had said. He stared at the ceiling. He stared at the floor. He was becoming adept at playing for time while he hung the various bits of information he collected on the relevant hooks in his mind.

"So," he said, speaking slowly and carefully, "are you saying I need more rehabilitation to get back to work? It will take longer than we thought?"

The doctors looked at each other and down at their charts. They had been filled in on how much of a struggle this might be. *Michael, we are telling you that you will never work again. I'm sorry.*

Mike held the sides of his chair, and his eyes lost focus and fell to the floor. "There have to be things I can do."

Michael. Michael, you've worked hard. Harder than anyone we've ever treated. You've made it further and done it faster than any person to come through here, but given the extent of the injuries you've sustained, returning to the level of function you maintained prior to the accident is not possible. It simply cannot be done. Now is the time to take what you have around you and build yourself a new life. You have a family who loves you and a lot of time ahead of you to enjoy all of the things you worked so hard for. Not many people get that chance.

It probably never occurred to them that the man in front of them never wanted a chance like that.

We kept it quiet for a while, to give him time to accept the news. We hoped that something new would start to filter into his mind, some new ambition that would take the place of everything he had built before.

He was quieter now. You'd ask him how he was, and he would say, "I just don't know what I'm going to do with myself." I could feel him slipping backwards as the goal he had pushed himself towards receded further from his vision and nothing took its place. There was nothing to self-actualize now. He stopped taking notes, stopped watching "Law & Order," stopped answering the phone. Everything stopped after that visit to the doctors. He could not bring himself to tell the firm or any of his old friends. Giving up the law to him was like giving up breathing.

I tried to get him to buy into my vision of what he should be doing, to let him know he could do anything he wanted now, all bets were off.

Mike, this is great. You have your health, for the most part. Now you have a chance to sit around and do anything you want. I know what I'd do.

What?

I'd just have a house. A great house. Maybe not a big house, but a great house. When people came over, a midget in a Beefeater costume would answer the door: 'May I get you a drink, sir?' Oh yeah.

That's it? That makes no sense.

No, Mike. That's not it. That's not even close to it. The thing you'll be going for, you'll be going for a sort of reflective detachment from anything, like you're barely paying attention. For you, nowadays, that's not going to be a problem. You're there, baby.

Thanks.

Don't thank me yet. Maybe this guest of yours, he walks out back, led along by this midget. You're out sitting in a chaise lounge, dressed like Hugh Hefner. You're reading the paper. But behind you, in full view of your guest, is an entire circus going on, just happening right on your lawn. There are people swinging from trapezes. There are fire-eaters. There's a ringmaster, there are elephants and lions and a fucking hippo. All of this is happening. But you're so goddamned stoked to be alive that you're just reading the paper and drinking a beer and not noticing a damn thing other than that beer and that paper. Know why?

Why?

Cause you're super fucking cool.

He wasn't buying it.

A new firm had signed him on less than a year before his accident. It was a big step for Mike to leave the firm he had spent twenty-five years and start again at a new one. His old firm was where his old man had started, and he had poured his guts into it. But there were only a few big rainmakers, and he thought they had gotten fat and lazy and would collapse someday, and his anger and frustration had burned a fair number of bridges around him.

He and his friend Joe negotiated a deal with a new firm. He was to build their litigation department and the opportunity had given him new life. He loved the place, they loved him. He had taken his old team with him so when he got there, he had friends already. It was like one big moveable feast for the old man, and this was Lawyerville now. He was running the show. They'd given him as much rope as he needed to hang as many people as it took to build out the team they wanted. Shit was smelling pretty good for a while.

When the accident came, they had still barely gotten to know him.

Say what you want about lawyers, but they take care of their people. The new firm could not have been better. They came to the hospital. They called. They offered money. They asked how he was. They patted your shoulder and told you how good your old man was, and how much they wanted him back. They meant it.

Nobody felt sorry for us now.

Everything has to give, though. These were patient men, but this was business, too. They'd bought the golden goose, and head injury or no head injury, they needed some golden eggs.

They called Mom and asked if they could come see him. We knew why. They liked Mike, but if the roles had been reversed, he would have done the exact same thing. They needed to know if he would ever come back; they had to get a look at their guy and see if this thing was salvageable.

The two managing partners came on a sunny spring day. On his desk both at home and in the office, Mike kept a miniature Superman. I had bought both of them for him in Florida when I was a kid, the kind of crap kid gift that often gets shoved in a drawer and forgotten. For a guy who was kind of a prick about everything, he had a thing about appreciating token gifts of my relative non-affection. In his closet, atop his cufflink drawer sat a giant gold belt buckle that read "Billy The Kid." I bought it for him at the church fair when I was six, knowing only that Mike enjoyed the odd Western and was probably a fan of Manifest Destiny.

My reason for purchasing these two miniature Supermen was unabashedly sincere: I knew it was how he liked to think of himself, and in way, I suppose I knew that giving him something like that would affirm for him that I had enough of a brain to catch on to that sort of thing. Not such a bad survival mechanism around our house.

And so growing up the Son of Superman gave me one rather mundane but occasionally useful superpower: to see the world as Mike did. I could look at any situation and know exactly the sarcastic, smirking, who-gives-a-shit-let's-get-down-to-business type of comment he would make.

I knew that if it had been another partner at that firm who had been hit on the head and had a lot of the firm's money tied up in his

future, they would have sent Mike Nolan to check things out, because
the man didn't have a sentimental bone in his body and would come
back with an answer: yes or no. They would walk into his office the
next day and there would be Mike, sitting at this desk. He'd look up
at them as they walked in, motion for them to sit down and deliver
the news: "Gentlemen, it's over." I was happy for us that no one like us
would be coming through the door for lunch that day.

Two senior partners came over, dressed like lawyers who were
never casual but did what they could when it came to putting on khaki
pants and a polo shirt. We all talked, sitting out on the deck with
lunch in front of us. It was the first time they had seen Mike since the
accident, and I'm sure their reaction was much like everyone else's:
nothing looks wrong with him. There were no scars, no casts, no obvious
physical problems at all. Not until five minutes passed, and then you
noticed the long silences. You noticed how he stared around, eyes set-
tling somewhere on the table or in the sky.

If you were a lawyer, accustomed to the rhythms and cues of language, you noticed something even before all of that: his repetition,
his lack of clarity, his pauses before speaking. They stayed for about an
hour, asking all of the polite questions, and engaging Mike in a few
conversations about the office.

"Are you looking forward to coming back to us, Mike?"

He stared down at his plate. "More than anything."

"Good."

I caught a look between them as they left, the kind of look a head
coach gives an assistant coach when a guy on the field keeps screwing
up. I could tell as we walked out that they would be on the phone back
to the office to give them the news. It would all be a formality now.

They had done everything they could for him. They had treated
him like gold. You could see it on their faces as they left. These guys
were no dummies. I could tell from their shared look as they walked
down the driveway to their cars. *He doesn't have it anymore.*

"We'll call you, Kathy. Look after our guy."

They pulled away, up the driveway, out onto the main road, and back to their world. She was looking at the ground.

"It's over," I said. She didn't say anything, and we walked inside. It was lonely there that night. We were out of The Club now, for the first time in our lives.

A month went by before they arranged the formal meeting at the firm, a lunch between Mike and the managing partners. They issued a formal statement to the firm. I was at work when one of his old team members forwarded it on to me. She talked about how sad she was, how awful a day it was for everyone. They mentioned how he had told them it was the toughest day of his life since the accident. When I called Mike, he didn't want to talk. I got one sentence out of him: "It's all gone."

It is still the saddest day of my life. They had taken all the fury and rage and passion away from him. People like him made everyone around them stand a little straighter, bust their asses a bit more, stay a little longer. A guy like that should explode somehow. Now I knew he would just fade away, and a bit of the rest of us would, too.

Chapter 19

A HISTORY OF LOVERS

I'm only here because Kathy saved my life. Out on the road, she
    pushed them to fly me to the hospital. They might not have done
    it if it weren't for her.

That's true, Mike. It almost didn't happen that way, you know. She
    almost wasn't there.

Did you know that?

Two weeks before the accident, she was going to leave him. He had
joined that new firm, and what had been a life spent obsessing about
the law and his clients and where the next deal was coming from had
downshifted into something else entirely. Mike was never home. It had
been years since they had taken a vacation, and that spring, telling her
that there was no way he would be able to get out of the office at all that
entire year, he offered to send her and a friend away somewhere.

Some people would look at that as a pretty good deal, but most
people didn't have to live with him. She saw which way things were
headed. As he started to get everything he had always wanted profes-
sionally, he seemed to want less and less of anything else. He barely
left work anymore. There were entire weekends at the beach with no
sight of him. He was working seven-day weeks, putting in punishing
days. This sort of thing usually did not end well, guys like him either
died at their desks or their wives left them, and most of the time, they
wouldn't notice if either happened.

We had all always been second bananas when it came to The Job,
but I think in some part of Kathy's mind, things were going to get

better when the kids were out of the house. Now we were gone, she had the place to herself, and he was away from the house more than ever. She had done all kinds of things to keep herself busy. She'd gone to school and gotten her degree in New York. She took classes at NYU. She tried hard to have a life away from his, but no matter what she did, she could never fill her days the way he could, and she wouldn't have wanted to.

So when he offered to send her away, she told him he could go to hell unless he came with her. Her friend could go with Kathy for a week, and he could come the second week. It had been years since they had gone away, and he goddamn owed her. He said he would.

"He works and makes all this money, and for what? We never do anything. We never go anywhere. The only time we ever have dinner together anymore is if we take out one of his clients. He's forgetting about me. So he can go screw if he thinks I'm sitting around for that shit." The old lady didn't mess around, and in our phone calls I could tell she was starting to get pretty pissed off with him.

Mike was forgetting about her. His life was pulling away from hers. Everything he had worked for during the last forty years was finally coming to him. He was the man at a firm that loved him, that respected him, that wanted to see more of him. On the rare occasions that I saw him, he was consumed with something else, checking his Blackberry or scribbling notes on a pad. You'd talk to him about something, and he'd nod along, and say, "That's great; give me a call and we'll talk about it," no matter what you'd just been talking about. He didn't care anymore. He didn't even care enough to say something nasty, and when you said something rotten to him, he just smiled and nodded. He wasn't in the room with you. His head was in a boardroom, and it was already tomorrow, and he was already winning the next battle.

Then things really fell apart. Kathy went on her trip to the Caribbean with her best friend. In the middle of the week, he called to tell her he wasn't coming, there was no way he could leave, things had really kicked off.

She called me on a Saturday.

"That son of a bitch."

"Hey, Kath. Where are you?"

"I'm home. He didn't come."

Mike had offered to pay for her to stick around with her friend, but she was having none of it. It was the worst move he could have made, and there would be worse to come. Over the next few months, his isolation from the rest of us would deepen. Calls to his office went unreturned. There were no more dinners together. There were no more haircuts. Getting on his schedule was impossible. His secretaries would take your message, but you never knew if he saw it. A few times, I'd get some random calls from him from the office, late at night on speakerphone.

Sometimes I'd still be in my office, and he'd ask what the hell was I still doing there. "You tell me, man. I must have gotten like this somehow."

"To hell with that, guy. Go on home. This is no kind of life."

"Tell me about it. I've got no one else to worry about, though. You do. You should do something nice for Kathy. Take her out. Do something, do it soon."

"I'm all over it."

But he wasn't. It got so that I dreaded talking to Kathy, because it was inevitably a conversation about something I could not solve, that I could barely help. I was in no position to offer any sound advice myself. I was about to start business school, I was not even thirty, and already I could see myself slipping into the same working ways, in a perversely lazy way. It was easier, it was easier to stay late. There was a certain comfort in an empty office, long after most of the people had gone home. Its strange loneliness made up for something, it defined you. You knew who you were. You knew you were becoming a "come in on Christmas" guy. That's how you referred to people who would drop anything for the job, "Oh, Jack? He's great. Come in on Christmas guy." If that call came to me while I was on vacation, I knew I'd be on the next plane back. Because I liked to work so much? No. Because it was how I liked to be. It was me.

Most of all, I was just my father's son.

That summer, it all went bad. Kathy had invested the time, but she was no fool, she saw it for what it was. He barely remembered his own birthday in June and when he was home, he was less and less there. There was no talking to him. Nothing worked. He started to pull away, and nothing was going back to the way it was, not for a long time. His old man had worked well into his eighties. At that rate, he would either make it that far or die trying. Things in the world move forward because of guys like that, guys for whom the horizon just gets further and further on down the road. If it didn't, things would stay the same or just break down. These were the workers, the fixers, the men with the plans. There would always be problems to solve, there would always be Things That Needed Them. They needed them.

In late July, she disappeared. I got a call from my littlest sister. Kathy was gone; no one had seen her in days. It was not unusual; people were always disappearing for days. We didn't talk enough for anyone to notice that anyone else was missing. We all lived alone now, in one way or another, none of us were really around, and certainly not around each other. But this was different. There had been a fight at the house, and four days later, she wasn't answering any phones, she wasn't talking to anyone, and she could be anywhere.

"Take it easy," I said. "She's been under a lot of pressure. Give her some time. She'll turn up." She was not swayed, but the call was over.

The following morning, she called again, and again that afternoon. "Listen. You have to let this thing play out." My sister was angry now.

That night, Mike called. He wanted to know where I was, and I told him.

"I need you to do something for me."

"Go."

"She's down at the apartment. I'm coming up from Washington. My secretary tipped her off like an idiot. Can you go down and keep her there?" I knew I could.

"Leave it with me." I left work, telling no one, and walked out into the thick Manhattan summer, the sun still bright but falling down towards New Jersey, down across Union Square, down University, to their apartment. She had to be there.

The doorman let me in, up to her place, and my first few knocks at the door were not answered. When she finally opened the door, I stepped back. She looked so small. In the month since I had seen her, she had seemed to shrink, to fade away ever so slightly. She shook her head and motioned me in.

"So I'm found."

"Are you OK?"

"No. I'm leaving him. I'm done with this."

I sat down on the couch, and she sat across from me.

"Don't stay. I want you to go. You're only going to try to talk me out of it, and I don't want to be talked out of it."

"I'm not going to do anything like that. I can't tell you how to do anything, Kath."

She lit cigarette after cigarette, smoking at a rate that far exceeded her usual intake. She had quit for fifteen years until she got breast cancer, and then took it up again, because she had always missed it, and once you'd had cancer, she figured, who gave a damn anyway. The woman had balls, I had to give her that. She would have had to in order to be around this long.

"You know how long I've stuck with this, and I guess this all seems a bit sudden, but this is it. This was supposed to be our summer, these were our years, after having you goddamn kids around for so long. This was going to be our time. But it won't be. This new job, this whole new life he's put together. None of those old conversations we had are going to happen."

"I know. Nobody thinks this has been easy, least of all me."

"I don't know what you think. Look, I know you came over here to be good. But I've got to get out of here. He's coming back up from Washington, and he'll probably come looking for me."

My phone was vibrating in my pocket, but I let it keep ringing. "Sit tight, Kath. I spoke to him. I doubt he's going to come here. He's got a lot going on; I think they got a big new case down there."

She nodded at my bullshit. "I bet he probably did. Good for him."

I wanted to let her go. He would have landed and would be racing here from the airport. Part of me wanted to sympathize with her, but the best of me couldn't see it. You pal around with lions, you can't complain when a few gazelles get eaten here and there. He had never advertised himself as a stay-at-home, let's-enjoy-the-passing-of-our-days kind of guy. I couldn't see how she had expected this to happen, how she thought that suddenly he would take the foot off the pedal late in life.

"Kath, stick around. Let's have a drink."

"I don't want a drink. I want to leave."

"To go where? Where are you going to go?"

"Somewhere else." She got up and walked back to her bedroom. I could hear her start to pack up. I turned on the stereo and closed the door to the hallway that led down to her room. I called Mike.

"So?" He answered.

"I've got it. How long?"

"Twenty minutes. My driver is Russian. We're flying." His voice was different. There was something in there that I'd never heard before, something like desperation. It was so rare to have him needing anyone else to do something for him. This was not a place he usually found himself in, and down through the streets and the tunnels, I could almost feel him willing himself up that highway and back into New York.

"OK. I can keep her here. But move it."

"Listen, pal. I know it's not easy. But this is the type of thing . . . this is the type of thing that guys like us come through on. Guys like us, we . . ."

I hated him then. I could see him there, in his suit and his cell phone, in a Town Car, speeding through the streets with no one to stop him. He was headed to just another meeting, another contract to negotiate, another bill to pay. He didn't see her like I did anymore. I stood there on the phone, and I was in on it, I had bought into it, become part of his world. Had it always been like this? Was there a piece of him that would have walked away at some point, the guy shooting hoops alone in Verona with his dead Marine friend in the ground, would he have done the right thing, would he have walked in to her, and said *Just go, just get out of here, walk away, while you can. I'll cover for you?* I felt a thousand miles down the road from where that kid on the bike on Route 35 had been going. All that work, and I was just here, just me, just the guy who would do it because it was the way we had always done it. Just moving the chains a few inches, realizing my own worthlessness.

"I'm so sick of guys like us." I closed the phone and walked towards her room. She was ready to go.

"Can I take you somewhere? I can walk with you. Why don't we sit tight and talk about this? We can work it out."

My mother was exhausted; she had barely slept. That was how she responded to stress, like me, she'd just stay up all night watching old movies and hope at some point she'd just pass out from it all.

"Let me leave. That's all I'm asking you. If he comes here, I'll never get out of here."

"OK. But I wouldn't mind having a chance to talk to you about it. I doubt he's coming here. I know you want all that stuff and that you banked on it. But you can wait a little longer. No one's going anywhere anytime soon. Sometimes you have to put things away. Things can just take a backseat to getting it done, and you can always come back to those things. Some things you should just be able to put in a box and have them be there when you're back. They should wait for you. You should wait for him. Don't take this away, just let him win this one thing."

"One thing? He's had a lifetime of winning, he just doesn't know it. He has me, he has all this stuff. It's my turn. It's my fucking turn now. He could have walked away from all of this shit with everything except this one thing, but he never will. It's not about me or you or any of our friends any more. He'll do this until he just drops dead at his desk, and the really hard thing is that's what he wants. He doesn't want weekends at the beach or a life together or to take me places. He wants to work until he falls down dead. And why? Why? So he can prove himself to his father? So he can be at the top of the pay list every year? We don't need another thing, and we haven't needed another thing for years. This isn't the icing anymore. This is the end."

I nodded at her. Without tackling her, keeping her around much longer was going to get harder. She walked around me. "You let yourself out. I'll call you."

Kathy opened the door, and there he was. She dropped her bag. Turning away from him at the door and back to me, she looked smaller than ever, but she must have known, she would have had to know. Sometimes it's not about hopes and dreams. Sometimes it just comes down to guys like us.

I left them there, like that, my role was over for now. I would not see them again until a Sunday, two weeks later, when they were down at the beach, still trying to put things back together, and he got on his bike and headed to Asbury Park.

Chapter 20

CHAINS, CHAINS, CHAINS

I was less than ten the first time I had the dream. I have had it a few times a year since then. It is always the same one, always the same person, always the same place.

There is a man in Joe's driveway, next to a silver car. He has come for a reason, not just a visit. From the moment it starts, I know he has come looking for something. He stands, staring at the house, hands at his side, looking up. He wears a suit and good shoes, and the sun reflects off of his glasses.

He walks slowly up the path, under the cedar trees that always kept it shaded. The front door is open, the old captain's head door-knocker looks back at him as he opens the screen door and walks into the foyer. He stops at the foot of the stairs, as if to gauge whether anyone is home. There is no one there but him, and he walks across the foyer and on up to the second floor. At the top of the stairs, light shines down from the big windows, streaming into the house. I think I can tell who he is, but he never looks back.

Is it Mike? It is for sure. I can see by the walk, by the way he takes the stairs with his big hands on the railing. He is too young to be Joe, and no one else moves like that. To his right is Jeanne and Joe's bedroom. The room looks out onto the bay, and you are taken aback by its size and by the big windows filled with calm blue water in the summer. In the winter, the water is grey, and always rougher from the wind blowing in from up north.

He stands by the windows, looking out on the pale water, dappled with tiny whitecaps. I see him touch the window itself, as if the water would be just on the other side of it. He holds his hand against the glass. Next to him stands a chest of drawers, brown wood that has been around for decades. I know it will smell of salt and wool before he opens it, and that it will be full of wool sweaters, because so many drawers in that house are full of them. In winter, we all wear them together, each one of them too big for us.

Carefully, he takes the sweaters out of the chest and stacks them neatly on an old rocking chair. His movements are slow and deliberate, like an actor who has rehearsed his movements and was going through them just as he had last night, and the night before, and the night before that.

The sunshine takes up the whole window, reflecting off of the bay, dancing across the ceiling in patterns. I realize that the sun is moving faster than it should, sinking down over the bay perceptibly, moving the shadows along the walls and across the carpet. His silhouette becomes dulled by the glare of the sun hitting the room. He is more of an outline of a man than a man.

Then I take my eyes off of the sun and see the gun in his hand. The one he always talked about, the one carried home from the war, wrapped in oilcloth all these years and kept in the bottom of that drawer, Uncle Eddie's old pistola. I see how he knows it, how he moves its parts slowly together, getting it ready. He sits on the edge of the bed, staring out of the big window onto the water. The sun is almost too bright now; I can hardly see anything but a trace of him against the window.

I saw him come here, I walked the path with him, I saw his hands get it ready. How else can it go for a man like that, everything according to The Plan. I watch him from across the room in his father's house, sitting straight up with his eyes on the water. When the pin hits the shell, I wake up, the report still ringing in my ears.

Lying in my bed, I roll towards my own window and feel a sick comfort. It is the only way out that made any sense for him. It's how I had always assumed he would leave the world. He would never let anyone else make the last move, not even God.

Mike loved to say how there was a difference between moving the chains and wearing them. I was not dumb enough to think that there was anything joyful or fun about it, but I always liked hearing that he knew the difference. There is something attractive in the guy who will drop it all and come back to the office, or leave it all out on the court when everyone else packs it in and admits it's over. There was a difference in being a killer and a robot, and he knew the difference.

Still, you could not have grown up around Mike and missed the quiet sadness of his life. The way he saw himself as the only one willing to do what needed to be done to move things along, to get it done, to leave it all behind—that's not something you watch and think that you would like to pick up and carry with you. Still, there was a steady nobility to it, and what I worried about most was that maybe that piece of him would be gone if he woke up from the coma. Maybe he would just be like every other schmo out there, accepting defeat, nodding his head, and going home to the wife to talk about how he had done his best. Maybe there would be no one to appreciate the guys who still saw reason in a life like that, because why do something beautiful if no one is around to value it?

Nobody feels sorry for us. At least, they should not. He always got what he wanted, and so did we.

There were small moments of quiet in which I allowed myself to feel sorry for us, and for myself a little. Life had been pretty good to me, and still there was the persistent whisper about how different things could have been if only a second or two could be changed. What if the conversation that started the argument at Joe's house had never come up? What if the kid that hit Mike started out a bit later? What if he had pedaled that bit faster?

I looked for Joe at my college graduation, and as strange as that may seem, there was part of me that believed he would show up. After Mike's accident, I'd phone his work number so I could hear them say "Mr. Nolan's office" before I hung up. For a second, those little bits of hope can make you feel like you can bring it all back and make life what it once was.

Then you step back, you see what you have, and you set that shit aside.

When I was a kid, Mike used to go straight up to the beach when he got home at night. He would come down to the house from work, drop his briefcase in the hall without a word to anyone, and walk straight out the door, onto the deck and then down to the beach. He'd stand there in his suit, looking like something out of an old Jackson Browne video, arms folded, pacing the beach, staring out over the ocean. I would sit on the deck, watching him watching the water, pacing like a prizefighter, waiting for something to come across the water to him.

On those nights I would look out over the sand and wonder about him. It was his secret strength in the world, the ability to be unknowable, to keep them all guessing. But I wanted to be an insider, and the more time he spent looking out to the horizon, the more I knew I was on the outs, along with everyone else. Even Kathy kept quiet about most of the things that you really wanted to know about. She would say, "He was never really like that," or "Oh, I can hardly remember back that far." The Old Man Omertà stretched out to everyone who had ever really known him. I thought about strolling down there on some of those nights, just asking if we could shoot the shit, about anything. Maybe he would even answer. But like a lot of things, I just never did.

He still went to the beach in the evenings, although now his days were taken up, not with meetings and endless phone calls about the law, but with Kids Corporation business. He'd gone back as the face of the place. Michaela stayed in charge, he would raise money and provide motivation, usually in the form of a rant about the injustice of how the kids in Newark lived, and sometimes in the form of phone calls to old clients and friends to ask if they wanted to do some good with him.

Now, I'd come off the train on Fridays, down from the city in a suit of my own and barrel through the house to stand on the deck and see him out on the edge of the water. People still wanted to talk to him, to see how he was doing, to say hello to the local miracle man. He didn't want to talk to them any more now than he did before the accident; he would stick a fishing pole into the sand next to him, so no one would ask him what it was he was doing there. He would stand on the beach long after everyone had left, taking in the fading twilight, arms folded, looking out across the water, watching like a soldier standing a post.

I'd walk down in my work shoes, not caring about the sand slowly working its way into the leather. Before, if you even went close to him, if you even wanted to see him, he'd know you were there, and he'd eyeball you all the way down the beach. You'd talk about work and what came next and where things were going, because they were always going, as sure as the water kept coming in. Michael wasn't like that anymore. These days there was only now; there was no then.

He had no plans, no destination, no particular place to be. As time went by, some things got harder, and some things got easier. For Kathy, there would always be the missing pieces of the guy she married. Their marriage had only gotten stronger, stripped of all the baggage of work and distraction. The years of armor he had put on in order to be Mike Nolan had fallen away.

For me, they were things he left on Route 35 in a summer that came and went years ago, in a time I could always recall but never quite get my head around. Everything was mixed up, and would stay this way until we were all gone and people forgot there was ever a lawyer who lived in that house at the end of the road to the beach who lost it all and got the best of it back. I liked him more than most people ever did throughout his whole life. He was like a gentle old retired philosophy professor now, spilling bits of wisdom, not really caring whether anyone heeded it or not.

While he stood there on the sand, the world going all purple around him from the setting sun, some random neighbor might arc his arm around and say, "Well, Mike. They can't take that away from you."

And Mike would look back at them and say, "Sure they can."

He knew more than most people how quickly it could all come and go, and as I walked down to him, I would recall the fear with which I used to approach him and smile a bit to myself at what had fallen away from us in the few short years since that accident. Now his face lit up when he saw you, in a way that let you know you mattered.

If he's not the same anymore, I don't want him to live. We were pretty wrong on that one. His layers of hurt and bitterness and sarcasm had washed away, and now all that was left was the guy who had always been there, but that none of us were ever allowed to see. All those times with him, at lunch or on the basketball court or watching him stare at the water, he was unknowable. Superman was dead, and in his place stood Mike Nolan.

"Hey, Mike." He turned around, wearing a Springsteen T-shirt and a "Women Want Me, Fish Fear Me" hat.

"Hey, guy. I'm so happy you're here."

"Thanks, Mike."

"You wanna go on a walk down the beach?"

"Maybe tomorrow. I just got down."

"How long did it take from the city?"

"I got the train. A couple hours. I had some beers on the way down."

"Oh, do they let you do that?"

I'd never thought about that before. "I don't know really. I just do it."

"There's a lot of that going around. You're just in time, I think I've figured my life out." This happened a lot now. He was forever figuring his life out, which meant he had no time to figure yours out anymore.

"No shit."

"Yes shit. I haven't figured out much. It's all just starting to make sense. Every day I'm just starting to get to the next thing."

"A lot has happened, old man."

He laughed. "Yes. And someday this could all be yours. Think about that."

"You worked for it."

He collected himself for a bit and stared out at the big boats drifting by on the horizon.

"All the stuff you told me. About how I was, the stories about me, about Joe, that was good. I feel like all the things people have said to me make it a little better. I can see myself a bit now, what I was, what I wanted. It doesn't make it any easier to have lost all of that. But I am happy that's not me anymore. Not at all."

"It's a good thing, Mike. Best thing we could have gotten."

"You think so? I hope so. I went and saw my old man. After those things you said about him, about how it ended, I had to know for myself."

"What did he say?"

He looked at the sand, and then at me.

"He said that some things were just not worth revisiting. I guess he meant me. That's OK. I can live with that. I live with everything else, I can live with that. When I was leaving, he told me something. He told me that night, that last night, that you went over there, you went and tried to talk him down. You were a man about it, and you fought for me. You walked away when he cut me loose. That you did what he would expect a son to do, even though he was your favorite, and you were his."

"He told you?"

"Yes. You did what I would expect a son would do, too. But it's more important that you did what a friend would do. You took my side, when it counted, and you didn't even have to tell me about it."

"I'm glad you know. I never would have told you."

"You were my friend. I was short on those. I'm shorter now."

I could not say anything for a while, and I put my hands in my suit pocket.

"You know, Mike, I used to have this funny thought. The thought was that someday Joe would die, and you and I, we would go to the funeral. We'd come down from the city, back to this place, and we would go to Our Lady of Peace, and he would be gone. Then, because you were the oldest, you and I would have to go to that house. Just the two of us. His lawyers would have the will, and they'd say you had to read it.

"We'd go into his office and sit there and read it and see what everybody got from him. Who won the raffle, that kind of thing. You wouldn't get anything, because that's the way it was. But I'd get that car. His Cadillac, which if I was going to get anything, that's what I would have wanted. We'd walk down to the garage, and it would be sitting there in the garage underneath its cover, and we'd go to pull the cover off, and I'd notice something in the corner.

"My old bike. That's what would be there, the one I rode down that night. I never did get it back after he drove me home. And you'd know right then what I'd done for you. You'd tell me I was your friend, and I'd leave that car and just ride back off on that bike, down Route 35, all the way back home.

"I used to think of that all the time."

"I like that."

I liked it, too.

"Do you do what you do because it's what I would have wanted? The old me?"

"I try not to think of it that way."

"Maybe you should. Maybe I wasted a lot of time. Maybe there's not a truck out waiting for everyone on every highway. Some guys get lucky."

"I know, Mike."

"Don't wait to get lucky."

"I won't."

"You are. You're waiting. I used to wait, I think. That's what it sounds like to me. You're running out the clock like you're up in The Big Game. You know, I'd come out here, Kathy says, and stare at the water every night. I'd love to know what it was I was doing. But I think I know. All that time, I was waiting. Waiting for that truck. It was like I must have known it was coming for me. And one way or another, it would all be over."

"Nothing's over, Mike."

"You come down here in your tie, and you think like I don't know. Careful. Be very careful. Time moves quick now."

"I will be."

"Don't wait," he said. "Remember everything. Remember me."

But I would wait. I knew it even I as squeezed his shoulder and started back up towards the house. I would forget. I would make the same mistakes all over again, just like he had. And it would be OK. There is nothing sad or given-up or wrong with that. It was OK to be what we were.

Mike no longer remembered the quiet pride of being there at night when the cleaning crew came and went, of sitting in offices and in circles of people getting it done, getting anything done, just not being fat or lazy or dumb, but mattering. I still wanted so badly to matter to someone, and if not someone, then something, anything. It was the worst day of his life when they told him he could not come to the office anymore. There would always be someone else to pick up the chains when you had dropped them. Sometimes it is fun to pretend that there would not be.

He wasn't that guy anymore, and good for him. His days being Superman were all behind him now, and he would have his time on the beach at sunset. He had it coming. So did I. Was it so wrong? Did every story have to end with the guy giving up working hard for all the things he wanted so he could drive off with the girl in a car with a "Just Married" sign on the back? Most stories don't end like that. You just get on with it and be happy for all you have. You can't waste time thinking about all the rest.

Too little, too late. Mike and his old man used to talk about those as being the four most terrible words in the English language. They meant you'd waited and not done enough when you could have, and that was about the most shameful thing they could imagine.

I left him there, walking back towards the house. I thought again of the things that had come and gone for us. There were little pockets of people, all down the beach, and I could see the big Ferris wheel way down in Seaside. They would be walking back up to the boardwalk now, into all those gorgeously trashy bars. There'd be music playing. In Point Pleasant, the kids would be running underneath what was left of the Big Rocks as the tide went out, chasing starfish as they walked out to sea, and their old man would be following behind them with a camera. On the courts across the highway, the guys from the neighborhood would be playing one last game before they went home and got ready for another Friday night at the beach. One town over from ours, Joe Nolan would be sitting on his deck looking out from the other side of our little island towards the bay. It would be cocktail time in that big old house, and some things hidden away there would stay hidden for good. In the garage, an old Cadillac, long remembered, sat under a green tarp, waiting for an old man and a young boy to shine her up and take her out.

There was still time. I looked down the beach and saw the old Thunderbird Hotel jutting out towards the ocean.

I called to him. "Dad? How far you think it is to the Thunderbird?"

"Far enough."

"OK, man. OK. Let's go."

ACKNOWLEDGMENTS

This book would not have been possible without my father, J. Michael Nolan, and I would not be half the man I am without him. Mike gave me a life loud with example, and I hope this book goes a small way towards making him aware of just how thankful so many of us are that he is alive.

Mike Nolan would not survive without my mother, Kathleen, and I would not be possible without her either. She gave me my love for reading, and softened me up enough to make me write. I am indebted to you, Mom.

Two people have been with me every step of the way in this venture. My Samoan attorney, Francis S. Barry, has been instrumental, from introducing me to my publisher, to offering detailed notes on writing, to always provoking me by doing things like publishing a book before I did. Frank is always the smartest guy in the room—at least the rooms I find myself in—and his counsel has been invaluable. My deepest thanks, Frank.

Friend-In-Chief, Patrick B. Barthel, has been my first phone call in every situation and has been the voice of reason throughout most of the poor choices I have made in my adult life. His advice and encouragement throughout this have been a big part of making it happen. Thanks, friend.

To Trish O'Hare, thank you for your advice, your persistence and your willingness to help see this through. You've been a great boss.

Finally, to Tracy McNulty, my favorite person in the world: thank you for getting me to the finish line.

These stories were my way of telling Mike where he came from and what he was like before he lost his memory in a devastating accident in August 2003. I make no claims to perfect accuracy; I can only promise that this is what I remember. Certain names have been changed to protect the guilty, as is customary in this type of situation.

Ten percent of the net royalties from the sale of *Guys Like Us* goes towards Kids Corporation, an institution providing after-school education and health services to thousands of kids in Newark, New Jersey.

Sean Nolan was raised in northern New Jersey. He spent his summers in Normandy Beach with his father, J. Michael Nolan, Jr., his mother, Kathleen Murray-Nolan, two sisters, Gwyneth and Michaela, and a brother, Antoine.

Like many, he eventually moved to New York City but could never escape the lure of his home state. Unlike most, he settled in Dublin, Ireland, where he has lived since 2007.

Sean Nolan received his bachelors degree in history from the University of Notre Dame, an M.B.A. from New York University and works in the financial sector.

He has not driven a car in eight years.